F-86 SABRE
THE OPERATIONAL RECORD

THE OPERATIONAL RECORD

Robert Jackson

Smithsonian Institution Press
Washington, D.C.

Published in the United States of America
by Smithsonian Institution Press

ISBN 1-56098-531-3

Library of Congress Catalog Number
available from the publisher

First published in United Kingdom
by Airlife Publishing Ltd.

Manufactured in the United Kingdom

00 99 98 97 96 95 94   5 4 3 2 1

Contents

Acknowledgements

I should like to acknowledge the help of the following people in preparing this book, especially with regard to the supply of photographs:

Sebastian Cox; Fred Gill; Phil Jacob; Philip Jarrett; Group Captain Ian Madelin; Ann Tilbury; A.A.B. Todd; Alan Todd.

Chapter 1
F-86 Development, 1945–50

IN THE spring of 1941, the idea that the gas turbine engine might have a worthwhile military application – a concept already well established in Germany and Great Britain, albeit after a very slow start in the latter – was still viewed with some scepticism in the United States. Nevertheless, interest in military circles was awakened to the extent that, on 17 March that year, the Chief of the Bureau of Aeronautics approved a proposal for establishing a special National Advisory Committee for Aeronautics (NACA) board 'to promptly review the status of jet propulsion and recommend plans for its application to flight and assisted take-off.'

In the following month, General H.H. Arnold – Chief of the US Army Air Corps and Deputy Chief of Staff for Air – went to England to assess for himself the state of jet engine development there; he was able to watch the first British jet aircraft, the Gloster-Whittle E.28/39, carrying out taxi trials and making a few short hops at Hucclecote, Gloucestershire. Suitably impressed by what he saw, Arnold contacted the State Department in Washington and suggested the initiation of high-level discussions that would lead to an agreement for the transfer of gas turbine technology from Britain to the United States. The agreement, finalized in September 1941, envisaged the manufacture of an initial batch of fifteen Whittle gas turbine engines by General Electric, and the construction of three airframes in which to test them. The choice of the General Electric Company was dictated by the fact that the other principal US aero-engine manufacturers such as Allison, Pratt & Whitney and Wright were too busy producing piston engines.

The firm selected to build the airframes was the Bell Aircraft Corporation of Buffalo, New York. Like General Electric, Bell was not heavily involved in America's new combat aircraft construction schemes, and another advantage was that the Corporation's factory was situated not far from General Electric's. Bell's management were enthusiastic about the idea and design work on the aircraft, which was allocated the designation XP-59A, was begun immediately. Shortly afterwards, a Whittle W.1 turbojet was flown to the United States in the bomb-bay of a B-24 Liberator, and transferred to General Electric's test facility at Lynn, Massachusetts. After a number of modifications, the engine – designated General Electric Type I-A – was bench-tested on 18 March 1942, the first of 30 such power plants to be constructed for the XP-59 programme and also the first tentative step on a road that was to lead the Corporation to the forefront of military aero-engine technology in the United States during the immediate post-war years.

The Bell XP-59A Airacomet flew for the first time from the USAAF's Muroc Bombing and Gunnery Range, southern California, on 1 October 1942, powered by two General Electric I-A turbojets of 1,250 lb thrust each. The prototype was joined at Muroc by two other XP-59As early in 1943, and while testing progressed with these, thirteen YP-59As were under construction at the Bell factory. In the meantime, General Electric continued with its efforts to uprate the basic I-A engine and encountered numerous problems in the process; as the engines became more powerful they became less reliable, and the latest in the series – the I-16, which was to have powered the YP-59As – had a life of less than fifty hours before needing a full overhaul. Problems such as this meant that the whole development programme slipped seriously behind schedule, and when the first two YP-59As flew in August and September 1943 they did so with less powerful I-14B engines.

There were other problems, too. When the Airacomet's armament of three 0.50 in machine-guns and a single 37 mm cannon was tested, the aircraft was found to be a very unstable gun platform at speeds higher than 290 mph. In addition, its maximum speed at 35,000 feet was only 390 mph, and it could be out-performed by both the piston-engined Republic P-47 Thunderbolt and Lockheed P-38 Lightning. In this failing it was not alone; in the summer of 1944, when the Gloster Meteor Mk I entered RAF service, the British jet aircraft too could be outflown by the later marks of Spitfire and the Hawker Tempest.

The Airacomet's performance during the aircraft's early test phase had already fallen a long way short of expectations, and in May 1943 the USAAF invited the Lockheed Aircraft Corporation to produce its own proposals for a jet fighter design to be powered by the de Havilland Halford H-1 Goblin turbojet, which had been selected for Britain's Vampire jet fighter. Lockheed did so, and in the remarkably short time of 141 days constructed a prototype which received the designation XP-80 and, later on, the name Shooting Star. This was taken to the Muroc facility, which was occupied by Lockheed personnel as the Bell Airacomet test programme wound down, and the aircraft flew for the first time on 8 January 1944.

In the late summer of 1944, while the XP-80 was undergoing its test programme, something happened that was to produce some radical changes of thought in the design and development of future combat aircraft: the Messerschmitt Me-262 jet fighter made its appearance over Europe in the fast bomber and interceptor roles. In

1943, the US Strategic Air Forces had suffered terrible losses on daylight bombing raids into Germany; the position had improved greatly when the North American P-51 Mustang escort fighter had become available in sufficient numbers to keep the *Luftwaffe*'s piston-engined fighters at bay, but the advent of the Me-262 threatened to reverse the situation. The Allied air forces adopted revised tactics to counter the Me-262 menace, but the real point was that the Germans had produced an *operational* jet fighter which, in the autumn of 1944, was far superior in aerodynamics and performance to anything the Allies were even projecting.

The secret of the Me-262's success was that, although the aircraft was advanced in concept, its designers had not attempted to push too far ahead into the unexplored realms of high-speed flight. It was originally estimated that the required performance could be obtained with two turbojet engines each developing 1,486 lb (680 kg) of static thrust, although this in fact proved inadequate and was raised to 1,980 lb (900 kg) static thrust in the operational Me-262A-1a. An all-metal stressed-skin construction was used, with formers and stringers for the fuselage, ribs and stringers for all flying surfaces and sheet-metal covering overall. The low-mounted wing had moderate sweepback (18° 32' on the leading edge) and was fitted with long-span ailerons, plain flaps inboard of the engines and full-length automatic leading edge slots. The outer sections of the latter were never satisfactory as they opened about one inch (25 mm) and brought about a considerable increase in drag at high speed. The fuselage was slender, with a rounded triangular cross-section.

The whole idea of sweeping an aircraft's wing is to delay the drag rise caused by the formation of shock waves. The swept-wing concept had been appreciated by German aerodynamicists since the mid-1930s, and by 1942 a considerable amount of research had gone into it. In the United States and Britain, however, the concept of the swept wing remained virtually unknown until the end of the war, when captured German research data became available for study. Early British and American jet aircraft were therefore of conventional straight-wing design, with a high-speed performance that was consequently limited.

In 1944, before German advanced aeronautical research data became available, the United States Army Air Force (USAAF), drawing on its combat experience in the European and Pacific theatres, issued specifications around four quite different fighter requirements. The first involved a medium-range day fighter that could also serve in the bomber escort and ground-attack roles; the second, a medium-range high-altitude interceptor capable of destroying any bomber a potential enemy might conceivably deploy over the next fifteen years or so; the third, a long-range 'penetration' fighter to fulfil the dual role of bomber escort and interdiction; and the fourth, a night and all-weather fighter.

The first of these requirements immediately awakened the interest of North American Aviation, Inc. (NAA), of Inglewood, California, manufacturers of the P-51 Mustang. At that time, the North American design team, headed by Ray Rice and Edgar Schmued, was working on the NA-134, a projected carrier-borne jet fighter for the US Navy. This, like the XP-59A and the XP-80, was of conventional straight-wing design and was well advanced, so North American offered a land-based version to meet the USAAF requirement under the Company designation NA-140.

On 18 May 1945, North American received a contract for the building of three NA-140 prototypes under the USAAF designation XP-86. On the same day, 100 NA-141s – production developments of the NA-134 naval jet fighter – were ordered for the US Navy as FJ-1s, although this order was subsequently reduced to thirty aircraft. While construction of three XFJ-1 prototypes got under way, design development of the XP-86 and FJ-1 proceeded in parallel.

A mock-up of the XP-86 was built and, in June 1945, was approved by the United States Air Force (USAF). There was, however, one worrying factor: according to North American's estimates, the XP-86 would have a maximum sea level speed of

The North American XFJ-1, progenitor of the swept-wing F-86 Sabre. Thirty FJ-1 Furies were built for the US Navy.

This shot of an F-86A Sabre illustrates the aircraft's rakish lines. The band around the rear fuselage shows the point where the tail section was removed for access to the engine.

574 mph at a gross weight of 11,500 lb, and this fell short of the USAF specification, which called for a maximum speed of 600 mph. The Republic Aviation Corporation was already building a jet fighter-bomber prototype, the XP-84 – later to be called the Thunderjet – whose estimated performance exceeded the XP-86's by a considerable margin, and the fear was that unless the XP-86's performance could be substantially improved, the USAF might not proceed with the project.

It was at this point that material on German research into high-speed flight, in particular swept-wing designs, became available for study by North American and other US aviation concerns. To investigate the concept further, North American's design team, under the leadership of Project Aerodynamicist L.P. Greene, carried out a series of wind tunnel tests with model wings at varying angles of sweep, and reached the conclusion that the XP-86's limiting Mach number could be raised to 0.875 by incorporating a wing swept at an optimum angle of thirty-five degrees. A complete Me-262 wing assembly was also sent to Los Angeles so that North American

could assess the effect of leading-edge slots on low-speed stability.

After completing more than a thousand wind tunnel tests, the North American team decided that the swept wing was the answer to the XP-86's performance problems. It was a bold decision, because at that time – in the autumn of 1945 – no aircraft possessing any marked degree of wing sweepback had yet flown successfully. In 1941, the Curtiss-Wright Corporation had begun flight testing an experimental swept-wing pusher design, the Model 24, and this had led to a fighter design of similar configuration, the XP-55 Ascender; but the aircraft had proved to be horribly unstable and two of the three prototypes had crashed. The XP-55 experience had helped to divert the thoughts of US designers from sweepback as a means of increasing fighter performance, but studies of the captured Me-262 data changed the picture radically. If performance estimates were correct, a swept-wing XP-86 would be nudging at the edge of sonic flight, a region as yet unexplored.

The redesigned XP-86 airframe, featuring

sweepback on all flying surfaces, was accepted by the USAF on 1 November 1945. It was a radically different aircraft from the original design; the sweeping of the wing, resulting in a rearward movement of the mean aerodynamic chord, had made it necessary to lengthen the fuselage by more than two feet, and this in turn had given rise to numerous other changes.

The aircraft that now emerged was a low-wing cantilever monoplane featuring a modified NACA 0012-64 wing section at the root and a 0011-64 section at the tip. The wing itself was notable for the heavy gauge of the materials used, particularly in the case of the skin. Although built as a centre section and two outer panels, the wing was made continuous through the fuselage by connecting the three sections with bolts and lock-on nuts round the perimeter of the joints. The torsion-box structure, which formed the centre section and housed one of the fuel tanks, comprised the two spars and the upper and lower double-skins, the stringers being within each of the latter. From the centre section to a point slightly inboard of the aileron each main wing panel was also a two-spar double-skin torsion box with very few ribs, tapered heavy-gauge skin, and closely spaced span-wise stringers in the form of hat-section extrusions. These panels contained fuel tanks.

Outboard of the sections described above, the structure had only a single, instead of a double skin, and the extreme tip portions were formed of plastic. Unlike the main torsion box, the leading edge structure, which was attached to the front spar, had many closely-spaced ribs; the trailing edge structure was essentially similar.

Each of the statically and aero-dynamically balanced ailerons was attached by three hinges, and there was a fabric seal between the rear wing spar and the aileron leading edge. Studies of the Me-262-type leading edge slots had shown these to be unsuitable, and instead the aircraft was fitted with Handley Page type automatic slats which extended over almost the whole wing leading edge, opening and retracting according to aircraft speed and attitude. To ensure their free working under any condition of wing distortion, each was in four loosely-jointed sections which moved forwards and downwards on tracks.

The slotted flaps were electrically operated over a range of 0–38 degrees and extended between the fuselage and each aileron. They were operated by a lever mounted beside the throttle and were inter-connected by a flexible shaft to ensure unified movement under normal conditions and – in the event of one actuator failing – to permit both flap sections to be operated. The half-flap position was determined by aligning a painted stripe on the flap leading edge with the trailing edge of the flap shroud.

The fuselage, of conventional stressed-skin construction, was built in two main sections to facilitate installation, inspection and removal of the turbojet. These two sections were joined by four bolts and featured quick-disconnectors for the wiring, control cables, hydraulic and fuel pipes. The rear fuselage was of simple construction, and the rearmost bay was of stainless steel. Speed brakes (also variously known as dive brakes and air brakes) were fitted on either side of the rear fuselage; each was in the form of a hinged panel which could be extended forwards or downwards into the air stream. The brakes were operated by electrically controlled hydraulic jacks, served by an engine-driven pump, and could be extended to any position from closed to open. In an emergency, a manual control permitted them to be closed by airflow load. At medium and high engine rpm the brakes took two seconds to open and about a second to close, and at idling rpm about six seconds to open and three seconds to close.

Both the fin and tailplane had a thirty-five-degree sweepback, and the tailplane was set at a ten-degree dihedral angle. The elevators were statically balanced and, like the tailplane, were of straightforward stressed-skin construction. The elevator and tailplane were geared together and moved differentially with movements of the control column to provide in-flight trim.

The XP-86's large clear-vision cockpit canopy moved fore and aft on tracks and was normally electrically operated by a three-position switch, although a cable system was installed for manual operation, in addition to the emergency ejection system. A loop aerial and cockpit pressure regulator were fixed in the canopy. The ejection seat was a North American development of a government-sponsored design.

Such, in broad outline, was the design of the XP-86. The swept-wing proposal received its final approval by the USAF on 28 February 1946, with acceptance of the re-worked design's cockpit mock-up, and early in August drawings were released to the North American engineering shops. In December 1946 the USAF placed a contract for thirty-three P-86A-1-NA aircraft, and on 8 August 1947 the first of two flying XP-86 prototypes (the third being a static test model) was completed and transferred to Muroc – now Edwards Air Force Base – for flight testing. After several weeks of assembly, systems testing and taxying trials, this aircraft, serialled 45-59597, was

An F-86A Sabre pictured on a test flight near the North American factory.

flown for the first time by North American test pilot George S. Welch on 1 October. The aircraft was powered by a 4,000 lb s.t. Chevrolet-built General Electric J-35-C-3 turbojet.

The XP-86's maiden flight lasted fifty minutes, and Welch spent forty of them trying to lower the nosewheel, which refused to lock in the down position. He finally succeeded, and the precious prototype touched down safely. Subsequent flights proceeded more smoothly, and Phase I testing of the XP-86, in which George Welch demonstrated that the aircraft generally conformed to specification, was completed in only thirty flying hours. The XP-86 was then handed over to the USAF for Phase II testing; this, the Air Force evaluation phase, was undertaken by Major Kenneth O. Chilstrom, who made eleven flights totalling ten hours seventeen minutes between 2 and 8 December 1947. Test flights were made at an all-up weight of 13,790 lb, which included 435 gallons of fuel, 7.7 gallons of oil, 241 lb of instrumentation installed in place of armament, and 180 lb of pilot weight. The aircraft was now fitted with an Allison-built J35-A-5 developing 3,920 lb s.t., and this gave the XP-86 a maximum speed of 599 mph at sea level, 618 mph at 14,000 feet, and 575 mph at 35,000 feet. In terms of Mach number, values ranged from 0.85 at 5,000 feet to 0.875 at 35,000 feet.

From the pilot's viewpoint, one delightful characteristic was the excellent all-round vision; another was the very low level of vibration – much lower, for example, than that experienced in the XP-80. Taxying presented no problems, and control at all times on the ground was very good. On take-off, however, the aircraft showed a tendency to sink, so the angle of attack was increased to thirteen degrees and maintained until safe flying speed was reached. Unstick speed was about 125 mph after a roll of 3,020 feet in still-air conditions, the aircraft clearing a fifty-foot

obstacle 4,410 feet from the start of the take-off run. Climb at sea level was 4,000 feet per minute, the XP-86 reaching 20,000 feet in six minutes twenty-four seconds and 30,000 feet in twelve minutes six seconds. Stalling characteristics at all altitudes were very good, a warning buffet being felt six knots above the stall, and recovery was immediate when airspeed was increased. Major Chilstrom had no hesitation in reporting that the XP-86 was superior to any fighter so far offered to the USAF.

Phase III testing began in January 1948. This involved speed trials at high Mach numbers, position error calibration, stick forces per G at fore and aft centre of gravity locations, accelerated longitudinal stability tests, rate of roll, speed/power calibrations, and control investigations conducted with various configurations. Flight testing was interrupted briefly after the pilot made a successful emergency landing following a nosewheel malfunction, the aircraft returning to the test programme in April.

The flight test programme showed that North American's wind tunnel calculations had indeed been correct, and that the critical Mach number of the XP-86's wing was 0.875. However, as the programme went ahead it was found that the aircraft developed no uncontrollable tendencies at super-critical Mach numbers, and on 26 April 1948 George Welch exceeded Mach unity in a shallow dive.

The second prototype, designated XF-86A (the 'P' fighter prefix having now been changed to 'F' in the United States Air Force) made its first flight on 18 May 1948, fitted with the more powerful General Electric J-47-GE-1 engine developing 4,850 lb s.t. This aircraft was, in fact, the first off the production line (serial 47-605), and the two that followed it, 606 and 607, were delivered to the USAF on 28 May 1948. These were the first F-86s to carry the armament of six .50-in machine-guns, three on either side of the forward fuselage. This gun, the M-3 model, had a rate of fire of 1,200 rounds per minute and ammunition supply was 267 rounds per gun. The guns

F-86A-5-NA 91241 was one of the third batch of 333 production aircraft.

were aimed with the aid of a Mk 18 sight, a lead computing device that included both a gyro and fixed sighting system. When a target was identified the span selector lever was set to correspond with the aircraft's span, and when the target appeared within a circle of six diamond images on the reflector the range control was rotated until the circle diameter was identical in size to the target. Within one second, the gunsight automatically computed the required lead and the guns were fired.

It was not long before the USAF had a chance to show the American public – and the world – what its new fighter could do. On 6 September 1948, it sent the third production F-86A, 47-608, to the National Air Races in Cleveland, Ohio, where Major Richard L. Johnson achieved an average speed of 666 mph over a three-kilometre course. This was sixteen mph faster than the world absolute speed record set up the year before by Major M.E. Carl, USMC, in a Douglas D-558 Skystreak; unfortunately, a number of mishaps with the photographic timing equipment (on one run the timers clocked the FJ-1 Fury chase aircraft by mistake) resulted in only three of the F-86A's runs being timed, and four timed runs were necessary for record purposes. However, a week later, on 15 September at Muroc, Major Johnson successfully raised the world air speed record to 670.84 mph (1,079.61 km/h). The record was to stand for just over four years.

While the first F-86As were in production, North American's design team had been working on a USAF requirement to endow the aircraft with larger tyres, and to accommodate these had carried out a number of modifications to the basic design, the most important of which was to increase the fuselage width by seven inches. The redesigned aircraft was designated F-86B, and 188 were ordered. In fact the F-86B never flew, because the USAF requirement was overtaken by technology, as higher-pressure tyres and new brake designs became available.

At North American's suggestion, the USAF transferred the F-86B contract to a new batch of F-86As bearing the designation F-86A-5-NA, to be fitted with the improved standard-size tyres. Each main undercarriage assembly now featured a 26 inch extra-high-pressure tyre and a Bendix multiple-disc hydraulic brake in a cast-magnesium wheel, while the steerable nosewheel assembly incorporated a thin-tyred twenty-two-inch wheel. Deliveries of the A-5 model began in late March 1949, when 48-129 was accepted by the USAF. The aircraft was fitted with an uprated J-47-GE-3 engine developing 5,200 lb s.t., and differed externally from the A-1 in having a V-shaped instead of a rounded windscreen and plastic plugs in the gun muzzles, the plugs replacing the flush-fitted automatic gun muzzle doors of earlier production aircraft. The automatic doors, which opened and closed when the machine-guns were fired, had proved to be prone to malfunction; the plastic plugs were simply blasted clear by the first shots.

Meanwhile, in January 1949, the USAF had begun accelerated service trials with the F-86A at Muroc, and in the following months the first operational F-86As were delivered to the 94th Squadron of the 1st Fighter Group at March Air Force Base (AFB), California. The 1st FG had previously operated F-80 Shooting Stars. Re-equipment of the Group's other two squadrons, the 27th and 71st, followed rapidly, and by the end of May 1949 the Group had taken delivery of eighty-three F-86As. The 1st Fighter Group was assigned to the Strategic Air Command, its role being the defence of Strategic Air Command (SAC) air bases. On 16 April

1950 it was re-designated the 1st Fighter-Interceptor Wing (FIW), and on 1 July it was transferred to Continental Air Command. Six months later it moved to Norton AFB, California, where it was de-activated on 6 February 1952.

When the 1st Fighter Group took delivery of its first F-86As, the North American fighter was an aircraft without a name. One of the Group's first acts was to sponsor a competition to find a suitable one. Seventy-eight names were submitted, and one stood out over the rest. On 4 March 1949, the North American F-86 was officially named the Sabre.

On 10 June 1948, the USAF had underpinned the confidence it had already displayed in the F-86 by ordering a third batch of 333 aircraft, designated F-86A-10, -15 and -20, powered by either the J-47-GE-7 or -13 turbojet. Deliveries of these aircraft, serialled 49-1007 to 49-1339, began in October 1949 and ended in December 1950, by which time four more USAF fighter Wings had equipped with the type. These were the 4th Wing (334th, 335th and 336th Squadrons); the 33rd Wing (58th, 59th and 60th Squadrons); the 56th Wing (61st, 62nd and 63rd Squadrons); and the 81st Wing (78th, 91st and 92nd Squadrons).

The three original F-86A Wings had very important assignments. The 1st Fighter Wing's task was to protect the aircraft production industries in the Los Angeles area, the 4th Fighter Wing was responsible for the air defence of the US capital, Washington, while the 81st Wing covered the nuclear weapons production facility at Los Alamos. Their mission became even more vital when, in May 1949, the Tupolev Tu-4 long-range bomber entered service with the Soviet *Dalnaya Aviatsiya*; later in the year, when it was learned that the Russians had detonated an atomic device, one-way attacks on American industrial centres by nuclear-armed Tu-4s became an alarming possibility.

In August 1951, the 81st Fighter Group (FG) deployed to Great Britain, the first squadron to arrive being the 116th Fighter-

Interceptor Squadron (FIS), newly assigned to the Group. This arrived at Shepherd's Grove, Suffolk, on 27 August; it was joined there shortly afterwards by the 92nd Squadron, while the 91st Squadron arrived at Bentwaters on 3 September. The arrival of the Sabres gave a much-needed boost to Britain's air defences.

From December 1950, the F-86A was replaced on the production line by the F-86E-1-NA, which was identical to the late production F-86A except for the installation of fully power-operated controls for improved manoeuvrability at high speeds. The most innovative feature of this system was the so-called 'flying tail' (more correctly described as a controllable horizontal tail). Though the rudder was cable-controlled, the ailerons and the all-moving tailplane-elevator assembly were operated solely by hydraulic power in response to control column movements. The system worked well, eliminating many of the undesirable effects of compressibility such as loss of control at high Mach numbers. The first production F-86E-1-NA was accepted for the USAF by Major Charles E. Yeager in March 1951, and 396 aircraft were built up to April 1952.

Long before this, political events had conspired to ensure that the Sabre made its mark on the history of air warfare. On 25 June 1950, Communist North Korean forces invaded the Republic of South Korea. Rapid reaction by American-led United Nations forces saved a desperate situation, and in September–October they launched strong counter-offensives supported by carrier-based aircraft and fighter-bombers – mainly F-51 Mustangs and F-80 Shooting Stars – of the US Fifth Air Force. The situation changed yet again during the last week of October, when the Chinese People's Republic committed massive ground forces to the battle, and early in November UN aircraft operating over North Korea were attacked by Russian-built MiG-15 jet fighters.

It was fortunate that the Chinese Communist Air Force made no determined effort to establish air superiority over north-western Korea during this crucial period, when the UN had no combat aircraft in the theatre capable of fighting the MiG-15 on equal terms. The USAF, to its credit, lost little time in taking steps to meet the enemy jet fighter menace. The initiative came from General Hoyt S. Vandenberg, the USAF Chief of Staff, who on 8 November 1950 – just a week after the MiGs first appeared in Korean skies – offered to release a wing each of F-86A Sabres and F-84E Thunderjets for duty in Korea. The offer was immediately accepted by Generals Earle E. Partridge and George E. Stratemeyer, respectively commanding the US Far East Air Forces (FEAF) and Fifth Air Force, and on that same day the 4th Fighter-Interceptor Wing and the 27th Fighter-Escort Wing were directed to prepare for an immediate overseas movement.

At this time, the 4th FIW was at New Castle County Airport, Wilmington, Delaware, where it was assigned to the Eastern Air Defense Force. The 27th FEW was at Bergstrom AFB, Austin, Texas, and was assigned to the Strategic Air Command. The aircraft of the two Wings were flown to San Diego, California, where in the two weeks after 14 November they were deck-loaded aboard aircraft carriers and a fast tanker. Advance personnel were sent to Japan by air, and the main contingents followed by rail and then by naval transport. Few of the personnel, both air and ground, knew how exacting the task ahead of them would be.

F-86A Sabre: Main Data
Span: 37 ft 1 in.
Length: 37 ft 6 in.
Height: 14 ft 7 in.
Weights:
  Empty, 10,093 lb.
  Take-off weight, 14,108 lb.
  With two 120-gallon drop tanks, 15,856 lb.
  With two 1,000 lb bombs, 16,223 lb.
Maximum speed:
  679 mph at sea level,
  601 mph at 35,000 ft.

Cruising speed: 533 mph.
Stalling speed (clean): 121 mph.
Maximum rate of climb: 7,470 ft/min. at sea
  level.
Time to 40,000 ft: 10.4 min.

Combat radius: 330 miles.
Service ceiling: 48,000 ft.
Engine: one General Electric J-47-GE-13
  turbojet of 5,200 lb s.t.

Chapter 2
First Encounters over the Yalu

THE URGENCY that accompanied the move of the 4th and 27th Wings to Korea created its own crop of problems. The biggest was that the aircraft had been loaded on to the aircraft carriers and tanker without really adequate water-proofing, and as a result most of them – especially those in passage on the tanker – suffered substantial corrosion damage from salt spray during the journey across the Pacific. As Colonel Ashley B. Packard, commanding the 27th Wing, wrote later: 'Two or three days allowed in properly preparing the aircraft for shipment would probably have saved another week at this end.'

Although the deployment of the two fighter Wings to the Far East was accomplished in record time, the situation in Korea had deteriorated rapidly while they were en route. General Partridge had planned to position the 4th Wing at Pyongyang Airfield and the 27th Wing at Kimpo, but in early December, with the two Wings assembled and combat-ready, such a deployment was no longer possible. The 27th Wing accordingly established a rear echelon at Itazuke, Japan, and deployed its Thunderjets to Taegu Airfield to begin armed reconnaissance and close support missions, while Colonel George F. Smith, commanding the 4th Wing, established a large rear echelon at Johnson Air Base, Honshu, and deployed pilots and

F-84 Thunderjets bound for Korea on the escort carrier USS *Sitkoh Bay*. The first F-86s also travelled on deck without adequate corrosion proofing, and suffered accordingly.

F-86A Sabres of the 4th Fighter-Interceptor Wing taking off from Iwakuni, Japan, en route for Korea. Note the identification bands (yellow and black) around the rear fuselage.

aircraft to Kimpo. This deployment, known as 'Detachment A' mainly comprised the Sabres and pilots of the 336th FIS. Kimpo was the only Korean airfield suitable for Sabre operation, and was already badly overcrowded.

On 15 December the 4th Wing began operations with a familiarization flight over North Korea, and on the 17th the Wing mounted its first offensive sweep of the war when four Sabres of the 336th FIS, each carrying two 120-gallon wing tanks to increase its range to 490 nautical miles, took off from Kimpo and headed north towards the Yalu River.

The American pilots, all of whom were highly experienced – some had already achieved the status of 'aces' by destroying five or more enemy aircraft in World War II – had given considerable thought to the tactics they would employ. They used the basic and well-tried 'finger four' battle formation which broke down into elements of two upon entering combat; the idea was to enter the patrol area at altitudes between 27,000 and 33,000 feet, just below contrail level, so that the pilots could easily spot hostile aircraft above them by their vapour trails. On this first combat mission, however, the Sabre pilots made a mistake that might have cost them dearly had they encountered skilled adversaries. As the distance between Kimpo and the Yalu was 430 miles and the pilots wanted to extend their patrol time, they entered the combat area at a leisurely, fuel-conserving speed of 0.62M, so that when the Sabre flight – led by Lt-Col Bruce H. Hinton – sighted a battle formation of four MiG-15s the F-86s were flying too slowly to achieve maximum effectiveness. Fortunately, the MiGs were below and climbing; their pilots doubtless believed that the American fighters were F-80s, otherwise they would almost certainly have climbed for altitude on their own side of the Yalu. They realized their mistake only when the Sabres came diving down on them, rapidly gaining speed, whereupon the MiGs broke away and dived for the safety of the river. They were too late. Colonel Hinton's element clung to the tail of the number two MiG and Hinton fired three four-second bursts from his six 0.50 in machine-guns. The enemy aircraft burst into flames and went into a slow spin. It was the first of 792 MiG-15s which were to be claimed as destroyed by Sabre pilots during the two and a half years of air combat that followed.

There were several more encounters between MiGs and Sabres during the next few days, but these were inconclusive and no casualties were suffered by either side. By this time both sides were quickly catching on to the other's tactics and rapidly taking steps to counter them. The Sabre's main drawback was its lack of endurance; patrolling at speeds of 0.85M and higher the Sabre pilots could afford to spend only twenty minutes in the vicinity of the Yalu before being forced to head for home with a safe margin of fuel. The MiG pilots quickly realized this limitation and exploited it to the fullest advantage, climbing to altitude north of the Yalu and then diving across at high speed to make their attack as the Sabres were withdrawing towards the end of their patrol. The Americans in turn began to mount patrols of sixteen aircraft, operating in four flights of four, which arrived in the combat area at various altitudes at intervals of five minutes. In this way the withdrawal of all but the last Sabre flight was adequately covered.

On 22 December, eight Sabres led by Lt-Col John C. Meyer, commanding the 4th Fighter-Interceptor Group (FIG) – one of the USAF's leading fighter pilots, with twenty-four victories in WW II – were on an offensive patrol at 30,000 feet south of the Yalu when they were engaged by fifteen-plus MiG-15s. In a dogfight lasting twenty minutes and ranging from high altitude to treetop level, the Sabre pilots destroyed six MiGs for the loss of one of their own number, Captain L.V. Bach. After this mauling the MiGs were absent from the sky for a week, and the next time they appeared, on 30 December, their pilots showed extreme caution in joining combat. On this occasion thirty-six MiGs crossed the Yalu and engaged sixteen Sabres, but the enemy quickly broke off the action and headed for home. The Sabre pilots claimed two MiG-15s damaged.

In all, the 4th Wing's Sabres carried out 234 offensive sorties during December 1950, claiming the destruction of eight MiGs together with two more probably destroyed and seven damaged for the loss of one of their own number. These early encounters left the Sabre pilots with the conviction that the two fighter types were more or less evenly matched; the slight advantages enjoyed by one over the other in various respects could almost be dismissed. What counted was the comparative skill of the pilots, and it was quickly apparent that in this respect the Americans enjoyed an overwhelming advantage. Time and again, superior tactics combined with superior training were to pay dividends for the United Nations in the air war over Korea.

Nevertheless, the Sabre pilots were almost always at a tactical disadvantage. Operating from their main base at Antung across the Yalu, the MiG pilots could select the time and position for their attacks. Moreover, the combination of high subsonic speeds and G forces permitted hardly any deflection shooting; the way to achieve a sure kill was from astern, but few pilots ever found themselves in this ideal situation more than once in an engagement. The Mk 18 gunsight mounted in the Sabre was found to be too erratic for accurate deflection shooting at indicated airspeeds of more than 500 knots, and the F-86's armament of .50 inch calibre machine-guns was allowing too many damaged MiGs to get away. With heavier-calibre, equally fast-firing guns and a radar-ranging gunsight the Sabre might have achieved many more kills than was the case.

On 2 January 1951, with Kimpo airfield threatened by the advance of the Chinese Communist Fourth Field Army, the 4th Wing's Sabres were evacuated to Japan. Their departure signalled a determined effort by General Liu Ya-Lou, the Commander-in-Chief of the Chinese People's Air Force (CPAF) to formulate plans that would lead to the establishment of communist air superiority over North

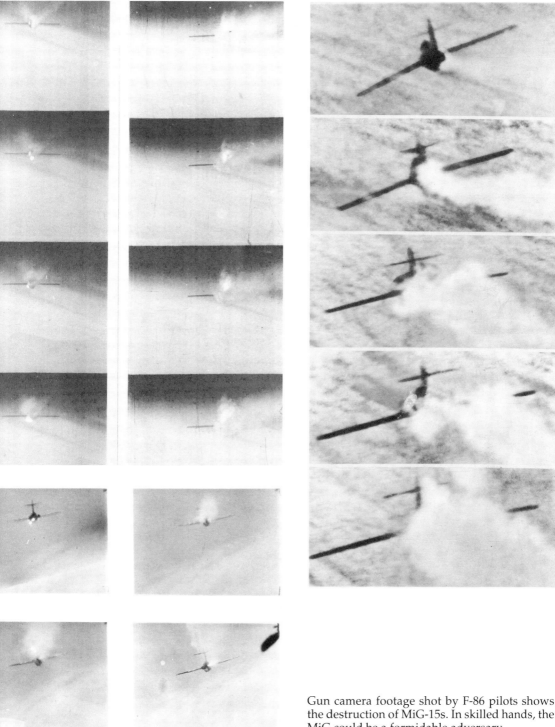

Gun camera footage shot by F-86 pilots shows the destruction of MiG-15s. In skilled hands, the MiG could be a formidable adversary.

Korea. Recognizing one principal draw-back – the limited combat radius of the MiG-15, the CPAF's most modern and numerous combat aircraft – Liu drew up a forward-looking air plan which envisaged, first of all, effecting a zone of air superiority over north-western Korea by reinforcing the MiG bases around Antung. The next step was to build or repair, under conditions of great secrecy, as many airfields as possible north of the 38th Parallel; these would then be garrisoned with MiGs and ground-attack aircraft ready for an all-out onslaught against the battered United Nations forces. This was to unfold in conjunction with a massive communist ground offensive which was to take place in May 1951.

Although the UN air offensive over northern Korea was sustained to some degree by F-80s and F-84s in January and February 1951, the absence of the Sabres meant that the Far East Air Forces had to adopt a policy of avoiding 'MiG Alley' as far as possible, so that operations in this area were confined mainly to fast photo-reconnaissance sorties by RF-80s.

This state of affairs was not to last for long. On 25 January UN forces launched a strong counter-offensive, Operation *Thunderbolt*, and by 10 February the UN 1st Corps had reached the Han River, retaking Seoul and Kimpo on the way. General Partridge immediately gave orders for the rehabilitation of Suwon, Seoul and Kimpo airfields, although it was obvious that it would be some time before the aviation engineers could get them fit for use by jet fighters. Nevertheless, the engineers reported that Suwon could be made serviceable enough to operate jet fighters in an emergency, and General Partridge was sufficiently encouraged by this news to authorize the redeployment of the 4th Wing's 334th FIS to Taegu on 22 February. On 26 February, the Fifth Air Force informed HQ FEAF that it was once more ready to escort B-29 bombers on inter-diction attacks on targets in north-western Korea, where the Superfortresses had

suffered heavy losses earlier in the campaign. This decision was based on the assumption that the 4th Wing's Sabres would be able to stage through Suwon and provide escort all the way to the Yalu. In fact the assumption was false; Suwon had taken such a battering that it would take months to get it fully serviceable, and operating out of Taegu the Sabres had just enough range to take them as far as Pyongyang. Despite this, the B-29 inter-diction programme went ahead, with F-80 Shooting Stars providing fighter escort, and it was a disaster. On the first mission, on 1 March 1951, the F-80s were forced to abandon the bombers because of fuel shortage when the B-29s were still some miles short of their objective, a bridge at Chongju. The bombers were attacked by nine MiG-15s and ten were damaged, three so severely that they barely managed to make emergency landings at Taegu.

On 10 March, following days and nights of non-stop work by the aviation engineers, Suwon airstrip was declared serviceable enough for use by Sabres, albeit with a certain element of risk. The 334th FIS accordingly moved up from Taegu, its place at the latter base being taken by the 336th FIS, fresh out from Japan. The 336th staged Sabre flights to Suwon each day to take part in the Yalu patrols.

With minor exceptions, the tactics used by the Sabres in their renewed patrols over north-western Korea were the same as those employed during December, the F-86 flights arriving in MiG Alley at intervals. The lead flight usually went to Sinuiju to stir up the MiGs across the river; if swirling dust on the runway at Antung indicated that MiGs were taking off, the Sabre leader would call out the fact over the radio telephone (R/T) and the other flights would converge on the sector. If an individual Sabre flight met a superior force of MiGs, the leader called 'Hey Rube' and made for Sinanju, where all flights joined up to engage the enemy.

The 4th Wing, with only two squadrons of Sabres in Korea, continued to fight at a tactical disadvantage, facing at least one air division with seventy-five MiGs at Antung. The Sabre screen was too thinly stretched. On 12 March, for example, while patrolling Sabres converged on a spot opposite where a formation of MiGs was reported to be assembling north of the Yalu, twelve more MiGs slipped across the river unobserved and bounced a flight of four F-80s of the 8th Fighter-Bomber Group (FBG). Fortunately the communist pilots appeared to be of low calibre; the Shooting Star pilots claimed four MiGs damaged and two more enemy fighters collided. Five days later, more 8th FBG Shooting Stars were again attacked by three MiGs which managed to slip through the Sabre screen. In the ensuing fight, one MiG and one F-80 were destroyed in a collision.

Meanwhile, following a pause after the disastrous mission of 1 March, FEAF Bomber Command had once again intensified its attacks on bridge targets south of the Yalu. On 23 March, twenty-two B-29s of the 19th and 307th Groups encountered only light AA fire during a successful attack on important rail bridges at Kogunyong and Chongju; the MiGs were airborne at the time but became engaged in a battle with forty-five Sabres of the 4th Wing several miles away, and none succeeded in getting through to the bombers. This attack was followed on 30 March by a raid on the bridges at Chongsongjin, Manpojin and Namsan-ni by thirty-six B-29s, with 4th Wing Sabres flying top cover and F-80s flying close support. The usual cloud of dust at Antung betrayed the presence of MiGs but most of them stayed over their own territory and only a few came over to attack B-29s of the 19th Group, badly damaging one bomber.

After that, low cloud over the Yalu brought about a temporary lull in bombing operations, but on 3 and 4 April both Sabres and MiGs were up in strength and the F-86 pilots claimed the destruction of four enemy fighters. On 6 April, with Sabres again providing top cover, B-29s attacked strategic bridges at Sinuiju and Uiju; on this occasion close escort was provided by forty-eight F-84 Thunderjets of the 27th Wing, operating out of Itazuke, Japan, and these fought a hot engagement with thirty MiG-15s. Only one MiG got through to destroy a B-29, and the F-84s claimed one MiG destroyed for no loss.

It was a different story on 12 April, when B-29s carried out another attack on the bridge at Sinuiju. Close escort was again provided by the 27th Wing, which put up thirty-nine aircraft, while the 4th Wing's Sabres flew top cover. With the target still several minutes' flying time away, the bomber formation was attacked by about fifty MiG-15s, which destroyed one B-29 of the 19th Group and damaged five others. This attack had scarcely ended when another was launched by twenty more MiGs, which scattered the Thunderjets as they dived through them on to the bombers. One B-29 of the 307th Group was shot down, and a second so severely damaged that it had to make a crash-landing at Suwon. On the credit side, the Sabre pilots claimed four MiGs destroyed and six damaged. The price of three B-29s destroyed – the one that crash-landed at Suwon was a complete write-off – and five damaged was too high, and on General Stratemeyer's orders all further B-29 raids in the Sinuiju area were called off until some really effective means of escorting the bombers could be found.

It was clear that the F-86 was the only UN aircraft really suited to escort and air superiority duties, but by the third week in April even the Sabre pilots were finding it increasingly difficult to establish a clear margin of superiority over their communist opponents. Flying discipline among the CPAF units had shown a marked improvement, and as they gained combat experience the MiG pilots became more aggressive and determined. They appeared to have abandoned the large, unwieldy formations of up to fifty aircraft, and instead were operating in battle formations of sixteen aircraft in four flights of four. The growing prowess of the CPAF fighter pilots was disturbing, for it manifested itself at a time when FEAF Bomber Command was about to launch a new series of air attacks on airfields in North Korea, which – as air reconnaissance showed – were now almost completely repaired. The attacks began on 17 April, and as it turned out fears that they would be contested by large numbers of MiGs proved to be unfounded. The MiGs were airborne all right, but they were successfully penned up near the Yalu by the 4th Wing's 334th and 336th Squadrons, which were now based side by side at Suwon. To counter the communists' new tactics the Sabres now operated in flights of six aircraft and timed their arrival in the combat area at closer intervals. This policy apparently took the CPAF pilots by surprise, because when thirty-six MiGs came across the river to attack twelve Sabres on 22 April – no doubt believing that they would enjoy numerical superiority for at least ten minutes – they were immediately bounced by a second formation of twelve Sabres coming along behind. Four MiGs were destroyed and four damaged; the remainder fled back across the Yalu.

The air battles of May 1951 saw the emergence of the first Sabre ace (although not the first jet fighter ace in history: six German Me-262 pilots had claimed that distinction in WW II). He was Captain James Jabara, a pilot with the 334th FIS. On 7 May, when his own squadron was rotated back to Japan, Jabara stayed on at Suwon to fly and fight with its replacement, the 335th FIS. by that time his score stood at four MiGs destroyed.

On 20 May, a large number of MiGs crossed the Yalu to engage twelve 4th Wing Sabres. Two more flights of Sabres, one of which included Jabara, were quickly summoned to the scene of the action. Jabara got on the tail of one of the enemy fighters and saw his bullets registering strikes on the MiG's wing and fuselage. He followed it down to 10,000 feet and saw the pilot eject. He climbed back to 25,000 feet and within a couple of minutes was fighting

with a second MiG, which he set on fire. He had time to watch it spin down in flames before being forced to break hard as a third MiG got on his own tail. He went into a long dive, losing the enemy fighter, and returned to base. His two victories were made all the more noteworthy by the fact that one of his wing tanks had refused to jettison, a circumstance that would have compelled most pilots to abandon the mission immediately. Other Sabre pilots claimed one MiG destroyed with one probable and five damaged. Jabara himself scored no further victories before the end of his current tour, but he returned to Korea later in the war and increased his score to fifteen.

After the battle of 20 May the MiGs avoided combat for ten days until the 31st, when twelve of them crossed the Yalu to attack two B-29s of the 19th Group heading for Sinuiju. One MiG was destroyed by B-29 gunners and two more were shot down by a flight of Sabres. The MiGs appeared again the following day, but this time they were more cautious; they waited until the Sabre escort turned for home, short of fuel, before crossing the river to attack four 98th Group B-29s which were bombing a bridge near Sinanju. One bomber was shot down and two more badly damaged, but the B-29 gunners claimed the destruction of a MiG and two more were downed by the pilots of a second Sabre flight which came up from the south.

The summer of 1951, which saw the collapse of the communists' planned major offensive and their expulsion from virtually the whole of South Korea, was characterized by a growing number of night attacks on UN airfields, carried out mainly by little Po-2 training biplanes. The 4th Wing's base at Suwon was a principal target, and one raid, carried out on the night of 16/17 June, produced spectacular results. On this occasion two Po-2s led by Lt La Woon Yung of the North Korean Air Force arrived over Suwon to find the airfield brightly lit, so that the two pilots could clearly see the 4th Wing's Sabres parked in their dispersals. La Woon Yung's two bombs straddled a flight of 335th Squadron F-86s, destroying one aircraft and damaging eight others, four of them seriously. In less than two minutes, one ageing biplane had inflicted more damage on the 4th Fighter-Interceptor Wing than had the MiG-15s in all their combats so far.

The Sabres, however, were not to have things all their own way in air combat for much longer. On 17 June, twenty-five MiG-15s came over the Yalu to attack two flights of 4th Wing Sabres on patrol. The Sabre pilots shot down one enemy fighter and damaged six others for no loss to themselves, but on their return to Suwon they reported that the MiG pilots had shown a high degree of skill and determination not previously encountered. The general opinion was that the enemy jets had been flown either by Russians or by extremely competent CPAF instructor pilots. The next day, forty MiG-15s that engaged thirty-two Sabres over the Yalu showed the same high calibre, but that did not prevent them from losing five of their number to the more experienced Americans. Nevertheless, one Sabre failed to return from this encounter – the second such loss in the Korean War. There was a third fierce air fight on the 19th, and this time the MiG pilots came out on top when they shot down one Sabre for no loss to themselves, although the 4th Wing pilots claimed four enemy fighters damaged.

The communists were sufficiently encouraged by this limited success to make a cautious foray over the border with Ilyushin Il-10 ground attack aircraft. On 20 June eight Il-10 fighter-bombers crossed the Yalu and headed for the island of Sinmi-do, which lay just off the Korean coast about seventy-five miles south-east of Sinuiju and which was being held by a small force of South Korean troops against repeated enemy attacks. The Il-10s were intercepted by Mustangs of the 18th Group, which destroyed two and damaged three, as well as shooting down one of six Yak-9 fighters which came to the assistance of the

Ilyushins. Then another Mustang flight arrived, this time escorted by two flights of Sabres – the latter reaching the scene just in time to intercept a dozen MiGs that came up from the direction of the Yalu. In the ensuing fight the Sabres damaged four MiGs, but one of them broke through to shoot down a Mustang.

Meanwhile, UN aircraft were hitting enemy airfields in North Korea hard by day and night, and it was in opposing these attacks that communist air activity over north-western Korea reached a new peak during the last days of June. On the 22nd, as Shooting Stars attacked Sinuiju airfield, Sabres and MiGs met overhead in an air battle that ended in the destruction of two MiGs and one F-86. It was a measure of the MiG pilots' new-found confidence that they now penetrated on occasions, either singly or in pairs and fitted with wing tanks, almost as far south as the 38th Parallel.

They also appeared, at last, to be exploiting the advantages of their aircraft, especially the MiG's ability to outclimb the Sabre and out-manoeuvre the American aircraft at high altitude. During this period UN pilots noted that the communists appeared to be experimenting with various types of tactics, including one which Sabre pilots nicknamed the 'Yo-Yo'. A large formation of MiGs would orbit the battle area at maximum ceiling, breaking off in small sections to make high-speed passes on the UN aircraft below and then zooming up to altitude again.

July 1951 was a bad month for the communist fighter pilots. On the 8th, twenty MiG pilots who crossed the river to attack Mustangs of the 18th Group strafing an airfield near Kangdong probably thought they had an easy engagement on their hands. Instead they ran into thirty-five Sabres of the 4th Wing, which shot down three of the enemy fighters. The next day, six MiG-15s which took off to intercept six B-29s over Sinanju lost one of their number to the Superfortress gunners and another to the Sabre escort. On the 11th, a fierce air battle developed south of Sinuiju when thirty MiGs attacked twenty-one F-80s; thirty-four Sabres joined the fight, and three MiGs were destroyed.

The following day, quite suddenly and without warning, the communist air offensive in Korea came to a halt – for the time being.

Chapter 3
Battle over the Yalu: Second Phase

BY THE summer of 1951, with the action in Korea settling down into a war of attrition and the ground being prepared for what would devolve into an apparently endless and fruitless series of communist-dominated armistice talks, the continued build-up of enemy air power in Manchuria had become a matter of grave concern. At this time the first-line strength of the Chinese People's Air Force stood at 1,050 combat aircraft, of which 690 were based in Manchuria, and several new airfields suitable for jet fighter operation were being built in the Antung area.

This airfield complex would shortly house some 300 MiG-15s, controlled by a well-equipped operations centre at Antung. Fighter controllers there were either Chinese or North Korean, but they were directed by teams of Russian advisers who were always in the background. Russian pilots were also very much in evidence in the combat units, where they usually assumed positions at flight- and squadron-commander level.

A careful assessment of the CPAF's order of battle, coupled with the knowledge that highly experienced Soviet aircrew were arriving in Manchuria in large numbers, pointed to the possibility that the communists might be planning a series of surprise attacks on UN air bases in Korea as a prelude to a new bid to gain air superiority.

On 10 June 1951 General Otto P. Weyland assumed command of the Far East Air Forces, and within a matter of hours he had contacted Washington with an urgent request for the deployment of four more jet fighter Wings to the Far East, two to bolster

The F-86E had full power-operated controls for improved manoeuvrability at high speeds. This variant was introduced into the Korean air war by the 51st FIW.

22

Japan's air defences in case the enemy launched air attacks against the large air bases there and the other two for deployment to Korea. The CPAF did not yet have the means to attack the Japanese bases, but there was a possibility that the Russians might supply Il-28 jet bombers for just such a purpose.

Washington, however, did not share Weyland's sense of urgency, taking the view that the communist air build-up was wholly defensive in nature. Moreover, there were fears that substantial United Nations air reinforcements in the Far East would be taken by the communists as a clear sign that the Allies were about to engage in unrestricted air warfare against China, destroying all hopes of early peace talks. The only gesture the US Joint Chiefs of Staff were prepared to make at this stage was to authorize the deployment of one F-84 Wing – the 116th FBW – to Japan. This was a bitter disappointment to General Weyland. At the time of his request there were only eighty-nine Sabres in the Far East, including forty-four in Korea, facing over 400 MiG-15s; Weyland wanted not only more Sabres, but new F-86E models to replace the F-86As with which the 4th Wing was then equipped. In fact, from July 1951 the USAF undertook to replace FEAF's F-86As with F-86Es on a one-for-one exchange basis, but this process was to continue for many months. The USAF's objection was that it would be impossible to provide Weyland with a complete Wing of F-86Es without depleting Air Defense Command, which was under strength and struggling to meet its commitments. The complacency of the immediate post-war years was having its effect, and it would be some time before the United States' technical prowess could match the Soviet Union's mass production of air superiority fighters.

By the end of July 1951, an evaluation of the pattern of communist air operations clearly indicated that the CPAF was about to make a new attempt to establish air superiority in MiG Alley. Exploiting their

A communist pilot ejects from his stricken MiG and floats towards the rugged North Korean terrain.

numerical superiority and the better altitude performance of their MiG-15s, the CPAF pilots evaded Sabre patrols at the Yalu and then continued southwards at altitudes above 35,000 feet as far as Pyongyang, where they turned back and descended to attack UN fighter-bombers which they sighted while en route homeward to Antung. There were several such attacks in August, although only one UN aircraft – an RF-80 – was damaged; four MiGs were destroyed by the Sabre screen.

On 1 September 1951, by which time the CPAF order of battle included 525 MiG-15s, the communists judged that the time was ripe to launch their new air offensive. The

MiGs began to appear in greater numbers than ever before, as many as ninety crossing the Yalu at one time. They were also better led, better organized and displayed superior tactics – clear evidence that the *honchos*, as the Soviet and Soviet-satellite pilots were nicknamed, were in control. During air battles on 8 and 9 September they used tactics hitherto untried in Korea. Some MiGs attacked in line astern, others used the Lufbery circle, and on one occasion four flights of MiGs made line-abreast head-on attacks in which all sixteen aircraft fired on a single Sabre. World War II veterans among the Sabre pilots had seen similar tactics before: they had been used by *Luftwaffe* fighters attacking American bomber formations over Europe.

During September 1951 the 4th Fighter-Interceptor Wing's pilots sighted 1,177 MiG sorties over North Korea and engaged 911 MiGs in combat, usually fighting against odds of three or four to one. Despite this, the Americans gave an excellent account of themselves. On 2 September, for example, twenty-two Sabres engaged forty-four MiGs in a thirty-minute air battle between Sinuiju and Pyongyang and destroyed four of them, and on 9 September, in a fight between twenty-eight Sabres and seventy MiGs, Captains Richard S. Becker and Ralph D. Gibson claimed a MiG apiece to become the second and third aces of the Korean conflict. Three F-86s were lost in these clashes.

By the end of September, the communist air forces were seriously interfering with the activities of Allied fighter-bombers striking at targets in north-western Korea, and General Weyland once again stressed the need to provide an additional Sabre Wing – or, failing this, to convert one of the existing F-80 Wings to F-86s. The USAF's response was blunt; supporting the existing Sabre Wing in the Far East was difficult enough – supporting a second was out of the question. As soon as he received this news, General Frank F. Everest – commanding the Fifth Air Force since 1

June 1951 – immediately ordered a halt to all fighter-bomber attacks on targets in MiG Alley. Instead, the fighter-bombers were to concentrate on a zone between Pyongyang and the Chongchon River.

Necessary though this decision was in the light of the growing communist challenge to Allied air superiority, it had dangerous implications. It meant that the enemy's airfield construction and rehabilitation programme in North Korea – brought to a standstill by comprehensive interdiction attacks during the spring and early summer – could now get under way again, and it soon became apparent that the communists were taking full advantage of the lull in UN fighter-bomber activity. During late September and early October reconnaissance aircraft located three major enemy airfields under construction inside a twenty-mile radius north of the Chongchon; each of these airfields could be defended by a fighter umbrella from one of the others, and it was plain that the communists planned to use them as a base in an attempt to establish air superiority as far south as Pyongyang.

Captain Richard S. Becker points to the spot where his bullets struck home on a MiG-15. Becker, a 4th FIW pilot, destroyed his fifth MiG on 9 September 1951.

24

The airfield complex was immediately targeted for a B-29 strike, but before this could take place it was essential that the Allies established a firm – if only temporary – measure of control of the sky over north-western Korea to prevent interference with the bombers. Beginning on 1 October, the 4th FIW accordingly stepped up its counter-air operations with the object of bringing the MiGs to battle and inflicting a severe defeat on them. The result was some of the bitterest fighting in the history of air warfare. During the first two weeks of September, although the odds against them steadily increased, the 4th FIW pilots claimed the destruction of nineteen MiGs, nine of them on the 16th alone. Attacks on Fifth Air Force fighter-bombers operating against rail targets between Sinuiju and Pyongyang decreased dramatically, although the MiGs still got through to them on several occasions. On 3 October, two MiG-15s were shot down by F-80s of the 8th FBW, the latter homeward bound from a rail cutting mission north of Kunu-ri.

The B-29 attacks on airfield targets began on 18 October, the bombers being escorted by F-84 Thunderjets and also by Gloster Meteor F.8s of No 77 Squadron, Royal Australian Air Force (RAAF). On 23 October, eight B-29s of the 307th Bombardment Wing (BW) rendezvoused with fifty-five Thunderjets of the 49th and 136th Wings and set out for the airfield at Namsi; ahead and higher up, thirty-four Sabres of the 4th Wing provided a screening force, quartering the sky south of the Yalu. Suddenly, over 100 MiGs crossed the river and within minutes the Sabres, effectively boxed in, were fighting for survival. While this dogfight – during which two MiGs were shot down – was in progress, fifty more MiGs approached the B-29 and Thunderjet formation and circled it at some distance, seemingly intent on drawing off the fighter escort. When the latter refused to take the bait the MiGs launched an all-out attack from every quarter, scattering the F-84 escort – one of which was shot down – and destroying three bombers. Four MiGs were claimed as destroyed, three by B-29 gunners and one by an F-84 pilot. The surviving bombers, all with severe battle damage, staggered back to emergency landings in Korea and Japan. It was FEAF Bomber Command's blackest day since the war began. On the following day, up to seventy MiGs broke through an escort of ten F-84s and sixteen Meteors to attack eight B-29s of the 98th BW, shooting one down and damaging most of the others, and on 27 October sixteen Meteors and thirty-two Thunderjets were again overwhelmed by ninety-five MiGs, which damaged four out of eight B-29s of the 19th BW attacking Sinanju bridge.

There was no doubt that the UN came very close to losing air superiority over North Korea in October 1951. During the month, UN pilots sighted 2,573 MiG sorties, and of these 2,166 engaged in combat with UN aircraft. United Nations fighter pilots or air gunners claimed to have destroyed thirty-two MiG-15s, the Sabres accounting for twenty-four for the loss of seven of their own number. By comparison with what they had achieved in preceding months, October's operations had been a success for the communists – so much so that they were encouraged to take the bold step of deploying combat aircraft south of the Yalu. Allied reconnaissance revealed twenty-six MiGs in revetments at Uiju and about sixty piston-engined aircraft – mostly La-9s, Il-10s and Tu-2s – at Sinuiju.

This was the gloomy picture that faced the USAF Chief of Staff, General Hoyt S. Vandenberg, when he flew to the Far East late in October to make a brief on-the-spot survey of the situation. After reviewing all available intelligence and talking with FEAF commanders, he came away convinced that General Weyland was right; the communist air threat was more serious than ever before. 'Almost overnight,' he commented later in a press statement, 'Communist China has become one of the major air powers of the world.'

Immediately on his return to the USA, General Vandenberg ordered the despatch of seventy-five F-86s, with air and ground crews and full supporting equipment, from the Air Defense Command to the Korean theatre. General Weyland planned to use these aircraft to re-equip the 51st Fighter-Interceptor Wing, which then had two squadrons of Shooting Stars, returning an equal number of F-80 crews to the USA in exchange. Transfer of the new batch of Sabres was carried out by sea – the aircraft this time being properly waterproofed – between 1 and 9 November. Meanwhile, the whole of the 4th FIW – including the 335th Squadron from Japan – was moved to Kimpo, which it shared with the Meteors of No 77 Squadron RAAF and the RB-26s of the 67th Tactical Reconnaissance Wing.

The arrival of the Sabre reinforcements was eagerly awaited, for in addition to their overwhelming numerical superiority the communist jet fighter squadrons now had another advantage. Allied pilots reported encounters with what appeared to be a greatly improved model of the MiG-15 with a far better all-round performance. The aircraft was in fact the MiG-15 *Bis* with an uprated VK-1 turbojet, the latest type to equip Soviet fighter squadrons, and in the

hands of a capable pilot it was more than a match for the F-86A.

In the meantime, the pilots of the 4th FIW – now under the command of Colonel Harrison R. Thyng, another WW II ace – were hard pressed to handle the MiG-15s which appeared over North Korea almost daily in November 1951. Up to eighty MiGs would cross the Yalu in co-ordinated 'trains' – the 'west coast train' and 'central train' and head southwards at over 35,000 feet to rendezvous over Pyongyang before returning towards Manchuria, detaching flights to attack Allied aircraft as the opportunity arose – the favourite targets being Sabres or fighter-bombers on their way home, short of fuel. As the MiG train approached the Yalu once more, the communist aircraft, now themselves low on fuel, more MiGs would cross the river to cover their withdrawal. These tactics meant that no United Nations fighter-bombers or reconnaissance aircraft could operate in the zone between Pyongyang and the border without interference from the enemy jets, and all reconnaissance flights into this area had to be escorted by Sabres, F-80s, F-84s or Meteors. RF-80 photojets were bounced by

F-86E-1-NA Sabre in which Captain Fred J. Ascani set up a new 100 km closed circuit air speed record of 1,023.038 km/h on 17 August 1951. The aircraft's nose was painted fluorescent red.

MiGs eighteen times during October and November, and although only one was lost several sorties often had to be made before a target was successfully photographed.

The 4th Wing's Sabres destroyed fourteen MiGs in November 1951. On the 18th, four Sabre pilots sighted twelve MiG-15s in dispersals on Uiju airfield, and while two of them provided top cover the other two, Captain Kenneth D. Chandler and Lt Dayton W. Ragland, made a low-level strafing attack that destroyed four MiGs and damaged several others. Four MiGs were shot down in a major air action on 27 November, one of them by Major Richard D. Creighton, who became the fourth jet ace of the Korean War.

Then came 30 November, and the biggest air combat success so far for the United Nations. That afternoon, thirty-one Sabres of the 4th FIW, led by Colonel Benjamin S. Preston, sighted a formation of twelve Tupolev Tu-2 bombers escorted by sixteen piston-engined La-9 fighters and sixteen MiG-15s heading for the island of Taehwa-do in the Yellow Sea, where ROK forces were fighting North Korean marines. Two of the 4th Wing's pilots, Major George A. Davis and Major Winton W. 'Bones' Marshall, became aces that day. Marshall later described the action:

'We entered the area right on schedule and sighted two large formations of MiG-15 jets coming across the Yalu River high above us. They were apparently out on their own fighter sweep, but they didn't come down on us. We held our formation and turned south in the hopes of cutting into them.

'Just then, Colonel Thyng called out bogies coming across the river dead ahead of us and about 10,000 feet below. He said he was going down to look and instructed me to cover them as the air above was filled with MiGs and there were more coming every minute.

'The bogies turned out to be a large formation of Tu-2 bombers and their fighter escort. There were several boxes of bombers in groups of three. They were surrounded by an escort of propeller-driven La-9 fighters. Another formation of MiGs was flying top cover. The Colonel called for a head-on pass by two squadrons of the Sabres. I came over the bombers just as the Sabres struck. It was better than the seat on the 50-yard line in a football game. As our fighters poured it on, the whole sky became alive with smoke and flame. It was really a sight – our boys scoring hits all over the bombers, and their fighters could do nothing because of the Sabres' superior speed.

'Right after the Sabres made their first pass on the bombers Colonel Preston called me and said "Bones, come on down and get 'em". We were in a perfect spot for an overhead pass. The entire squadron went over on its back and came in on the bombers from six o'clock high, right on the Mach. As we dived, the remaining bombers turned their guns on us and their fighters nosed towards us in an attempt to turn us from the battle. The whole area was alive with bullets. The bombers that hadn't been hit still held a tight formation and straight course. They were like sitting ducks.

'I lined up the bomber on the right side of the last box. My first burst set him afire. As I continued to fire, he fell out of formation and the crew began baling out. Then two La-9s came into my sights and I gave the leader a short burst from my 0.50 calibres. He seemed to come apart at the seams and dropped like a stone to the ocean.

'Our first pass on the Tu-2s was over in a matter of seconds. I glanced to see if my squadron was still with me and then turned into them again for another pass. It gave me a thrill, for this was the first bomber formation I'd ever tangled with. By this time the area was so crowded with fighters I had to weave in and out between them to get in position for another pass. Finally, I squared away on the lead box and fired my remaining ammunition into one of them. He started smoking as my bursts cut into his wings and fuselage . . . I pulled away.'

When the battle ended, the Sabres had destroyed eight Tu-2s, three La-9s and a MiG-15. Three of the bombers and the MiG had been shot down by Major George Davis.

While the 4th FIW held the line against growing odds, the 51st Fighter-Interceptor Wing had been preparing to convert its two F-80 squadrons to Sabres, and in preparation for the change Colonel Francis S. Gabreski assumed command of the Wing at Suwon on 6 November. Gabreski had destroyed 28 German aircraft while flying P-47 Thunderbolts in WW II, and he already had two MiGs to his credit in Korea. He was to down another four and a half MiGs while commanding the 51st FIW, the half MiG shared with another WW II ace, Major Bill Whisner. On 19 November the 51st FIW transferred its F-80s to the 8th Fighter-Bomber Wing (FBW), and after a short working-up period flew its first Sabre combat missions on 1 December 1951.

FEAF now had 165 Sabres in the theatre, of which 127 were committed to combat in Korea. The reinforcements came only just in time, for in December the pace of the enemy air offensive showed no sign of slackening and the communist pilots continued to display a high level of aggression. On 1 December, for example, more than forty MiGs launched vicious attacks on fourteen Meteors of No 77 Sqn RAAF; the Australian pilots destroyed two MiGs but lost three of their own number. During the next few days the MiGs also shot down two F-80s and an F-84, but to achieve these successes they had to descend to lower altitudes, where they were outclassed by the Sabres.

This was well illustrated on 2 and 4 December, when the Sabre pilots claimed ten MiGs, five on each day. These combats gave the pilots of the 51st FIW first chance

to draw blood, two MiGs falling to their guns. On 5 December two more MiGs were shot down by Major George Davis, commanding the 334th FIS, and on 13 December Davis claimed another four MiGs in the course of a series of air battles that flared up along the Yalu. On that day the 4th Wing's Sabres met 145 MiG-15s in combat and destroyed thirteen of them. After that, serious encounters became more sporadic; the MiGs continued to appear over North Korea in large numbers, but they stayed at high altitude and showed little inclination to fight. Only three more MiGs were destroyed by the end of December; one by the 4th Wing on the 14th and the others by the 51st Wing on the 15th and 28th.

Despite very strenuous efforts, the communists had again failed to wrest air superiority from the United Nations in the autumn and winter of 1951, and some time in the middle of December the CPAF/NKAF air command evidently implemented a new operational plan. During the latter part of the month, United Nations Command Intelligence reported that the CPAF had moved several air divisions from the Antung airfield complex to bases in China proper, replacing them with new units. The 'pincer-and-envelopment' tactics were abandoned; large numbers of MiGs continued to enter North Korean airspace in 'trains', but they generally did so over the Sui-ho Reservoir, patrolled unaggressively at altitudes between 35,000 and 42,000 feet as far south as the Chongchon River, then turned northwards to Antung. Apart from routine maintenance work at Uiju, Sinuiju, Pyongyang and Sariwon, the communists also abandoned serious efforts to build or rehabilitate airfields in North Korea.

The only logical explanation for this behaviour was that the enemy had given up hope of attaining air superiority, and was instead using Korea as a training ground. After December 1951, Sabre pilots began to notice a definite pattern to enemy air operations. It appeared that the MiGs

The F-86 Sabre was a valuable workhorse at Edwards AFB Flight Test Center throughout the 1950s. This E model saw considerable service as a chase aircraft.

operating at very high altitude were flown by raw pilots; as these gained proficiency they came down to lower levels, became more aggressive, and gradually engaged the Sabres using fairly well-planned tactics. When this 'class' reached a peak of operational proficiency it was rotated and a new one came in, repeating the process. In this way, the communists were seeking to train the maximum number of pilots and to test their equipment and organization against their principal enemy, the United States Air Force.

To the pilots of the 4th and 51st FIWs, the early months of 1952 were times of bitter frustration; they were desperately eager to get to grips with the MiGs, but the MiGs did not want to fight. In one sense perhaps it was just as well, because the un-programmed conversion of the 51st FIW to Sabres had placed an enormous strain on logistical support, which the USAF had earlier claimed was inadequate to support even one Sabre Wing in combat. Proof of this was in the unserviceability rate in January 1952, when on average 45 per cent of the Sabres were out of commission: 16.6 per cent for want of spares, and 25.9 per cent because of maintenance problems.

With two Sabre Wings now operational, the requirement for external fuel tanks rose by 500 per cent in four months, so that supplies of these tanks in the Far East theatre were practically exhausted by January 1952. Throughout that month, Sabre pilots flew combat patrols with only one tank. They reached their patrol times by way of compensation, but even so many pilots barely made it home for dead-stick landings, their fuel having run out. Emergency supplies were flown by C-124 Globemaster aircraft direct from the contractors in the USA to the combat area, but the Sabre Wings still had to reduce their combat sorties to a minimum in February 1952. The USAF Air Materiel Command launched a crash programme called *Peter Rabbit* to raise stocks of spares to an acceptable level, and by April 1952 the unserviceability rate for lack of spares was down to 2.4 per cent.

Another major problem was the provision of trained combat pilots in adequate numbers. Until the autumn of 1951 the line had been held by the 4th Wing's highly qualified career pilots, many of whom had vast combat experience, but when these were rotated at the 100-mission mark they left a huge gap that was only partly filled by an influx of pilots whose previous combat experience had been gained in multi-engined transports and bombers, so that they had to be converted to the Sabre under conditions that were, to say the least, undesirable. The replacement pilots kept on arriving early in 1952, when aircraft serviceability was at its lowest, and there were simply not enough aircraft to go round. As a result, Sabre pilots were able to fly, on average, only ten combat missions per month, which was not enough to permit them to maintain combat proficiency. The situation improved in March, when increased serviceability permitted more combat operations, and the Sabre Wings began to receive young fighter pilots fresh from training in the United States.

There remained the problem of getting to grips with the high-flying MiGs. This was particularly acute in the case of the 4th Wing, which, although it had begun to receive new model F-86Es, was still equipped mainly with F-86As and which claimed only five MiGs destroyed in January 1952. The 51st Wing, equipped entirely with F-86Es, fared better; its pilots claimed twenty-five kills during the month, many of them on the 6th and 25th. On these days the 51st FIW's pilots entered the combat area at 45,000 feet, enabling them to make high stern attacks on MiGs which they sighted lower down. The MiGs were now crossing the Yalu in forces of up to 200 aircraft flying at high Mach numbers – up to 0.99M on occasions.

February 1952 was a month of sadness for the 4th Wing, for it saw the loss of Major George Davis. On the 10th, Davis was leading eighteen Sabres on an escort mission to Kunu-ri when he sighted a large number of contrails north-west of the Yalu, heading in his direction. Leaving the main body of the Sabres to defend the fighter-bombers he sped towards the bogies, accompanied by his wingman, with the intention of breaking up the threat before it developed. The two Sabres engaged twelve MiGs and apparently took them completely by surprise. Davis shot down two of them and was pressing home an attack on a third when his aircraft was hit and crashed into a mountainside. He was subsequently awarded a posthumous Congressional Medal of Honor. His score at the time of his death stood at fourteen enemy aircraft destroyed, a record that was not bettered until the following year.

On 25 February, Major William T. Whisner of the 51st FIW destroyed his fifth MiG to become the Wing's first ace and the seventh of the Korean War. Whisner, who commanded the 25th FIS, already had twenty-one kills in WW II.

Early in March 1952 the MiG pilots suddenly turned aggressive again. Although some sorties continued to cross the Yalu at high altitude and avoid combat, others showed a willingness to fight in elements of two, four and six aircraft lower down. Coming out of Manchuria at 40,000 feet and high Mach, they would make turning sweeps to lower levels in MiG Alley in search of UN fighter-bombers before making a high-speed dash for home at low level. The MiG pilots had now learned to stay below contrail level whenever possible, so that spotting them in time became something of a problem.

In general, the Sabre formations entered the combat area stacked down from 40,000 feet to give themselves a good chance of engaging the MiGs. The tactics worked well; in the eight weeks up to the end of April 1952 the F-86 pilots claimed eighty-three MiGs for the loss of six Sabres. The MiG-15s also shot down two F-84s and an F-80. It was hardly surprising that several 4th and 51st Wing Sabre pilots found themselves in the 'ace' category during these two months, with five or more enemy aircraft to their credit. They included Captain Iven C. Kincheloe, who also destroyed four Yak-9s on the ground in two separate strafing attacks on Sinuiju airfield on 22 April and 4 May; Captains Robert H. Moore and Robert J. Love, and Major Bill Wescott. They were joined in May by Captain Robert T. Latshaw, Major Donald

E. Adams, Lieutenant James H. Kasler and Colonel Harrison R. Thyng. James Kasler later increased his score to six. Colonel Harry Thyng, who – among other types – had flown Spitfires with the 31st Fighter Group in North Africa, already had eleven enemy aircraft to his credit in WW II. He was perhaps the most diversified of all the American aces, his victories including German, Italian, Japanese and French aircraft – the latter a Vichy Dewoitine D.520 – as well as Russian-built MiGs. He eventually retired from the USAF with the rank of Brigadier-General.

In May 1952, it became apparent that communist air policy had again taken a new turn. Training flights over North Korea ceased altogether, and communist air commitment was greatly reduced. United Nations pilots encountered only 620 MiG-15 sorties during the month, and from the wide variety of markings displayed by the MiGs it seemed that the enemy was using his best pilots, drawn from many different air units. For the first time, the United Nations had clear evidence that the communists were making extensive use of radar in carrying out their interceptions. On numerous occasions in May, Allied fighter-bombers were bounced by MiGs which, having been helped to avoid the Sabre screen by ground radar, dropped down through a cloud layer to find their targets.

The two Sabre Wings flew the Korean War's peak monthly total of 5,190 F-86 sorties in May 1952, shooting down twenty-seven MiG-15s and five Yak-9s for the loss of five of their own number. The MiGs also claimed three F-84s and a Mustang, two of the Thunderjets in the course of an engagement between twelve MiGs and twenty-four F-84s of the 49th FBW over Sonchon on 17 May. Realizing that the MiGs were now entering North Korea at altitudes of between 15,000 and 35,000 feet, the Sabres lowered the altitudes of their barrier patrols and provided top cover for fighter-bomber strikes in MiG Alley. On 13 May, in a pioneer dive-bombing attack with 1,000 lb bombs, Sabres of the 4th Wing knocked out Sinuiju's runway, proving that the F-86 was an acceptable aircraft for this type of operation. It underlined the fact that the communists could not hope to garrison their North Korean airfields without first gaining air superiority, and this, in the spring of 1952, they had again failed to achieve.

Chapter 4
Stalemate on the Ground, Victory in the Air

IN THE summer of 1952, United Nations Intelligence once again established a number of alarming developments across the Manchurian border. By the middle of the year, the strength of the Chinese People's Air Force stood at twenty-two air divisions, comprising 1,800 aircraft of which 1,000 were jet types. In addition, there was a further potential menace in that Soviet air strength in the Far East had risen to over 5,300 aircraft. Not the least disturbing news was that the CPAF had received about 100 Ilyushin Il-28 jet bombers, most of which were based in Manchuria.

The communists were also hard at work on a new airfield complex across the Yalu in the summer of 1952, and had set up about twenty-five radar stations that were able to provide coverage of air space up to and even beyond the 38th Parallel. There were also a dozen GCI stations, mostly situated in the west coast area, which gave effective fighter control in all weathers over a seventy-mile radius.

From the beginning of June 1952, the communists showed a hitherto absent ability to co-ordinate all their air defence measures in a new challenge to Allied air superiority over north-western Korea. Night fighters were active against B-29 sorties, while the MiG pilots were showing much greater proficiency in daytime battles with the Sabres. This did not prevent the Sabre pilots from claiming twenty MiGs destroyed for the loss of three of their own number in June; one Sabre pilot, Lt James F. Low of the 4th Wing, joined the ranks of the jet aces during the month by destroying his fifth enemy aircraft.

The MiGs were up in strength on 4 July, when fifty of them crossed the Yalu to intercept Allied fighter-bombers attacking targets at Sakchu. All the fighter-bombers escaped, but the MiGs lost thirteen of their number in a fight with the Sabre escort, two F-86s also being lost. Six more MiGs were added to the Sabres' score during the remainder of the month, making a total of nineteen. In all, four Sabres failed to return from the July engagements. United Nations pilots destroyed thirty-five MiGs in air combat during August, six of them shot down in a fight between thirty-five Sabres and fifty-two MiGs on the 6th. Two Sabres were lost. Yet another ace was added to the United Nations list: Captain Clifford D. Jolley, who shot down a MiG-15 on the 8th to bring his score to five.

September turned out to be the most hectic month so far. The MiG pilots showed aggressive intentions right from the first day, when several penetrated as far as Haeju to attack Allied fighter-bombers. Once again, the communist pilots threw away their advantage with poor gunnery and teamwork, and only succeeded in damaging one Mustang. On the 4th, thirteen MiGs and four Sabres were lost in seventeen separate air battles; one of the MiGs was shot down by Major Frederick C. Blesse of the 4th Wing, who before September was out would have three more to his credit. On the 9th, no fewer than 175 MiGs crossed the river to intercept Thunderjets which were attacking the North Korean Military Academy at Sakchu, a favourite target since early in August. The Sabre screen was not strong enough to cope with all of them and some broke through to shoot down three fighter-bombers. Two more Thunderjets and six Sabres were

The first F-86F conversion seen on a test flight from Inglewood. With its '6–3' leading edge, the F-86F could meet the MiG-15Bis on equal terms at high altitude.

destroyed in air combat during the rest of the month, but the UN pilots claimed a record total of sixty-three MiGs. On 21 September Captain Robinson Risner destroyed his fifth MiG near Sinuiju to become the Korean War's twentieth jet ace.

Their heavy losses in September made the communist pilots more cautious during the following month. Most of the work was done by the *honchos*, the veteran pilots; while the large MiG formations remained at 40,000 feet or even higher – on occasions MiGs were tracked at 53,000 feet – the experienced flight and squadron commanders would dive down and attack targets of opportunity. Alternatively, groups of twelve or twenty-four MiGs would seek out four-Sabre flights and attempt to box them in.

Both Sabre Wings were now operating a mixture of F-86Es and F-86Fs, the first examples of the latter having arrived in June. These were assigned to the 39th Squadron of the 18th FIW, which was immediately transferred to the 51st Wing to bring it up to a three-squadron establishment. The Wings now used their two Sabre models to good effect in countering the enemy's tactics, operating in flights of six or eight aircraft with the higher-powered F-86F at 40,000 feet plus and the F-86Es working lower down. In October, the Sabres destroyed twenty-seven MiGs, which in turn claimed only four F-86s and one Thunderjet – although they also scored successes against Naval aircraft operating in the Wonsan area, shooting down two Skyraiders and a Corsair.

Although November 1952 was a fairly quiet month as far as air combat was concerned – the communist fighter units encountered during previous weeks apparently having been withdrawn for a rest and replaced by new ones whose time was mostly taken up with operational training – the UN Sabre pilots nevertheless managed to increase their total score by twenty-eight MiGs for the loss of only four F-86s. The month saw three new Sabre aces: Colonel Royal N. Baker and Captain

Leonard W. Lilley, both of the 4th Wing, and Captain Cecil G. Foster of the 51st Wing.

The MiGs enjoyed an increased success rate in December, but it had little to do with the fighting ability of individual pilots. About the middle of the month the communists suddenly launched a variation of their tactics; a formation of MiGs would by-pass the Sabre screen and head southwards to the Chongchon River, where they would lie in wait for Sabres going home short of fuel. A number of Sabre pilots found themselves trapped in this way, and at least four had to bale out when their fuel ran out. Apart from that, only two Sabres were lost in actual air combat during the month, while UN pilots claimed twenty-eight MiGs.

The MiGs again made extensive use of the revised tactics in January 1953, but homegoing Sabres were generally able to keep out of trouble by flying a curve over the Yellow Sea. Early in the month, UN Sabre pilots reported that although most of the MiGs – presumably still engaged in one of their habitual training cycles – still remained at over 40,000 feet, some of the MiG units they were meeting showed a skill that matched their own. These units – whose aircraft were reportedly camouflaged pale blue underneath, with copper upper surfaces and bearing plain red stars – almost always stayed to fight and used every trick in the book. Once or twice, Sabre pilots caught a glimpse of their opponents' features; even disguised by oxygen masks and helmets, it was plain that they were Caucasian, not Asian. The United Nations claimed thirty-seven kills for the loss of one Sabre during January, but most of the victories were scored by high-flying F-86Fs whose pilots were lucky enough to engage the enemy novices. Two 51st Wing pilots, Captain Dolphin D. Overton III and Captain Harold E. Fischer, both became aces during the month, Overton destroying five MiGs in just four missions. On the last day of the month, a Tu-2 bomber – the first encountered for a

Fine air-to-air shot of an F-86F in company with another type which, in the reconnaissance role, saw service in Korea: the North American B-45 Tornado.

year – was shot down by Lt Raymond J. Kinsey of the 4th FIW.

In January 1953 the 18th Fighter-Bomber Wing (FBW), which included No 2 Squadron, South African Air Force (SAAF), began its long-awaited conversion from Mustangs to F-86Fs at Osan-ni airfield. The first three Sabres arrived on 28 January, the day after Mustang operations ceased, and conversion training began on 3 February. On 25 February the Wing flew its first combat mission with Sabres, four F-86Fs

An F-86F launches a salvo of high-velocity aircraft rockets. The F-86F was widely used in the ground-attack role by the 18th FBW in the latter months of the Korean War.

accompanying a fighter sweep to the Yalu. However, Colonel Frank S. Perego, the Wing commander, was not satisfied with the progress that many of the ex-Mustang pilots were making, so he reassigned them to other Fifth Air Force duties. The deficiency was made good by the arrival of replacement pilots from the United States, and the Wing's three squadrons – No 2 SAAF, the 12th and the 67th – were up to their task by early April.

It had originally been intended that the 8th FBW was to convert to Sabres after the 18th FBW, but delays in the arrival of F-86Fs meant that both Wings underwent conversion at about the same time. The 8th FBW, converting from F-80C Shooting Stars, experienced fewer transitional problems than the 18th FBW. Conversion began at Suwon on 22 February 1953, and re-equipment of the 35th and 36th Squadrons was completed by early April. The 80th Squadron continued operations with its F-80s until 30 April, when it too

equipped with Sabres. The 8th FBW flew its first F-86 mission on 7 April, when four Sabres joined a Yalu sweep.

It was the 8th Wing, in fact, that flew the first F-86F fighter-bomber mission, on 13 April, and on 14 April the 18th Wing also made its fighter-bomber debut with the new type. Except for the addition of bomb shackles, a modification to its gun-bomb-rocket sight, and special 200-gallon drop tanks, the F-86F fighter-bomber was no different from the interceptor, and any fears that it would not adequately fill its new role were soon dismissed. After a month's combat operations, General Weyland predicted that the F-86F would be an excellent fighter-bomber. 'I consider it a particularly desirable improvement in our tactical force,' he said, 'because of its versatility in accomplishing the three phases of the tactical air force mission: that of gaining and maintaining air superiority, interdiction, and close air support.' After four months in combat, the Fifth Air Force described the Sabre as the most suitable fighter-bomber employed in Korea. It displayed a superior ability to survive, was a stable gun and bomb platform, had no airfield or operating problems not peculiar to other jets, and possessed satisfactory stability when carrying external ordnance at high altitudes. When fitted with 200-gallon external tanks, the Sabre could carry two 1,000 lb bombs to a radius of action of 360 nautical miles.

On the air superiority front, February 1953 saw the start of a friendly tussle for the position of leading jet fighter ace before the Korean hostilities ended. Major James Jabara, with six MiGs to his credit during his earlier tour with the 4th Wing, was back in Korea, and his score was already beginning to climb. The total to beat was fourteen enemy aircraft destroyed – the score of the late George Davis before his untimely death the year before – and Jabara was coming up fast. But so were a number of other pilots, and one in particular stood out.

Captain Joseph McConnell had been turned down for pilot training during WW II, and had flown a couple of tours as a navigator on B-24s. It was only after the war that he was accepted as a pilot, finally emerging as one of the first batch of USAF Shooting Star pilots in February 1948. When the Korean War broke out McConnell was in Alaska; he immediately applied for combat duty, but instead of being transferred to Korea he was sent to George Air Force Base in California. It was not until the autumn of 1952 that he eventually got his wish and joined the 51st Fighter-Interceptor Wing at Kimpo.

He destroyed his first MiG on 14 January 1953. Just over a month later, by which time he was a flight commander with the 51st Wing's 16th Squadron, his score had risen to five and he was racing almost neck-and-neck with Captain Manuel J. Fernandez of the 4th Wing. Fernandez downed four more MiGs in March, bringing his score to ten, while McConnell accounted for three more, making a total of eight. Three other pilots also became aces during the month;

one was Major James P. Hagerstrom of the 18th FBW, and the others were Colonel James Johnson and Lt-Col George L. Jones, both of the 4th Wing.

In March 1953 the 4th Wing played host to a project called *Gun Val*, in which eight F-86F Sabres equipped with 20 mm cannon were sent to Korea for combat evaluation. The cannon showed promise for the future, but the trials showed that the installation was not yet ready for combat. During late 1952 and early 1953 much thought was given to improving the Sabre's overall combat performance; one scheme, tested in the autumn of 1952 and rejected by the Fifth Air Force, involved fitting the Sabre with externally-attached solid-fuel rockets which were supposed to give the F-86 an extra burst of speed for overtaking a MiG.

The real boost to the performance of the F-86F came with the installation of solid wing leading edges, which were tested by the Air Research and Development Command. While manoeuvring at high altitude, Sabre pilots had been unable to use the maximum permissible rate of turn without encountering transonic buffeting and risking pulling out the leading edge slats. Considering this problem, North American test pilot George Welch suggested removal of the slats and extension of the wing leading edges. The new wing leading edge increased chord by six inches at the root and three inches at the tip and, consequently, became known as the 6-3 leading edge. The absence of the beneficial effects of the slats on the airflow at low speeds was partly compensated for by the use of small wing fences at approximately 70 per cent span, but the modification raised stalling speed and produced a yaw-and-roll effect before the stall, making a faster landing approach necessary. Nevertheless, these penalties were considered to be far outweighed by the operational advantages accruing from the wing modification, all-round performance being improved and 1.5G at 0.92M at 30,000 feet.

Fifty sets of the new leading edges were shipped to Korea for the modification of F-86Fs, the programme being kept under strict security wraps. The improvement was immediately apparent. The modified F-86F could out-turn the MiG-15 in high altitude combat, and the lower drag from the smoother aerodynamic shape resulted in slightly higher level flight speeds at all altitudes. The changes were at once incorporated on the production lines and more conversion kits shipped to Korea. Not until the conflict had ended were details of the 6-3 leading edge revealed.

With the knowledge that the F-86F was now more than a match for the MiG-15 at all altitudes, General Glenn O. Barcus, commanding the Fifth Air Force since May 1952, was now ready to 'turn the tigers loose'. To goad the enemy into action, Fifth AF drew up a leaflet which asked 'Where is the Communist Air Force?' and dropped it in large numbers on enemy troop concentrations. There was no apparent reaction in April; only 1,622 MiG sorties were sighted, and in sporadic combat the Sabres destroyed twenty-seven enemy fighters for the loss of four of their own number. One of the latter was Captain Harold E. Fischer, the 51st Wing ace, whose score then stood at ten MiGs. He was taken prisoner. Joseph McConnell's Sabre was also badly hit during a fight on 12 April, but he ejected safely and was rescued by an H-5 helicopter of the 3rd Air Rescue Squadron. He was back in action within 24 hours, shooting down his ninth MiG, and he got his tenth on 24 April. He was now level with Captain Fernandez, but that state of affairs was not to last; on 27 April Fernandez shot down his eleventh enemy fighter.

As leaflet drops by the Fifth Air Force and B-29s had produced no tangible result, FEAF planned to prod the enemy into action by mounting a spectacular attack on Radio Pyongyang's facility on Communism's red letter day – the First of May. Unknown to higher command, General Barcus had been flying combat missions with the 51st Wing for the past two months, and on 1 May he flew as airborne commander for the Pyongyang Radio attack. While the 4th and 51st Wings flew screening and covering operations, the 8th and 18th FBWs passed over Pyongyang as though heading out for a Yalu patrol, then suddenly let down to bomb the radio station and its power supply. The attack took the defences completely by surprise and only one Sabre was damaged by AA fire. Circling over Pyongyang and using a radio frequency which the communists were known to monitor, General Barcus identified himself and promised: 'We will be back every time you broadcast filthy lies about the Fifth Air Force'.

The attack represented the utmost loss of face to the enemy air forces, but their anticipated reaction was thwarted by bad weather that persisted for a week. From then on the MiGs were very much in evidence, but now there was a difference. For the past few months, many of the MiGs encountered had carried the plain red star of Soviet Russia, but now they bore the markings of either Communist China or North Korea. It has been suggested that the Russians decided to pull out their fighter contingents following a United Nations offer of a 100,000 dollar reward to any communist pilot who defected and brought a MiG-15 along with him, but it is far more likely that an agreement had already been reached between the Soviet Union and China to bring the Korean hostilities to an end, given a reasonable face-saving period, and that the Russians, having learned all they wanted to learn from nearly three years of jet combat, saw little point in involving themselves further. They had, after all, had ample opportunity to examine every type of Allied aircraft involved in the war, many of them coming down virtually intact in enemy territory.

Whatever the facts, the enemy pilots who now faced the United Nations were no longer *honchos*. They were keen and aggressive enough, but they were inexperienced and they paid for it with their lives. The mission of the Fifth Air Force's Sabre Wings was now to seek and destroy, rather than screen and protect, and they modified their tactics accordingly. The Sabres now used up to 98 per cent of their power while awaiting combat; the higher speeds reduced the time they could stay on patrol, but it made catching MiGs easier, and if a MiG attacked, its rate of closure was slower. Between 8 and 31 May Sabre pilots sighted 1,507 MiGs, engaged 537 of them, and destroyed fifty-six for the loss of only one F-86. In seven instances the MiGs went into inadvertent spins in combat manoeuvres above 35,000 feet, and in most cases their pilots ejected. In other engagements, the enemy pilots baled out as soon as a Sabre opened fire.

The Fifth Air Force's fighter pilots threw everything into the MiG hunt in May 1953. Old aces added to their scores and a new ace was created. On 10 May Captain Fernandez destroyed a MiG and shared in the destruction of another. With a score of fourteen and a half his lead seemed assured, but by 18 May Joseph McConnell had shot down six more MiGs to bring his personal score to sixteen – a jet combat record that remains unbroken. Fernandez never had a chance to get his revenge, for on 19 May both pilots were relieved from combat duty. Sadly, McConnell was killed on 24 August 1954, while testing a new F-86H Sabre.

May 1953 saw the return to combat of Major James Jabara, the original Korean jet ace with a score of seven aircraft destroyed. On the 26th, Jabara shot down his eighth and ninth MiGs; just over a month later he was to become a triple jet ace by destroying his fifteenth enemy aircraft, moving into second place behind McConnell. The air battles of May also saw Lt-Col George I. Ruddell, commanding the 51st Wing's 39th Squadron, shoot down his fifth MiG.

It was as though both sides knew, in June 1953, that the great battle for supremacy high above the Yalu was drawing to a close. Sabres and MiGs hurled themselves at one another in a series of battles that resulted in the destruction of seventy-seven enemy fighters, with a further eleven probably destroyed and forty-one damaged. There were no Allied losses. To the Sabre pilots, it seemed that the enemy was really scraping the barrel; often, when a Sabre got on a MiG's tail, the enemy pilot took no evasive action at all, but merely crouched as low as possible in the cockpit and held a steady course while the F-86's fire chopped his aircraft to pieces, relying on the thick armour plate at the rear of the cockpit to keep the bullets from him before he ejected. Sixteen of the Sabres' total kills were claimed on the last day of the month – a new record. The June battles saw the emergence of five new aces: Lt-Col Vermont Garrison, Captain Lonnie R. Moore and Captain Ralph S. Parr of the 4th Wing, and Colonel Robert P. Baldwin and Lt Henry Buttelman of the 51st.

The eagerness of the up-and-coming aces to add to their scores during July was frustrated by bad weather during the early part of the month, but on the 16th the weather cleared and the F-86s were detailed to escort a series of fighter-bomber missions against targets in north-west Korea. The F-86F fighter-bombers of the 8th and 18th Wings were active in these operations; on 18 July they attacked the airfields at Uiju and Sinuiju, where reconnaissance had revealed enemy aircraft in some numbers, and there were several follow-on attacks during the next five days. The attacks destroyed twenty-one MiG-15s at Uiju and six other aircraft at Sinuiju; the surviving machines at the latter base were flown back over the Manchurian border.

By 27 July, all North Korean airfields were once again listed as unserviceable by FEAF Intelligence. What was not known at the time was that the enemy, taking advantage of the bad weather at the beginning of the month, had flown no fewer than 200 MiG-15s and piston-engined combat aircraft into Uiju and dispersed them in the countryside adjoining the highway between Uiju and Sinuiju. These aircraft would form the basis of a re-constituted North Korean Air Force immediately after the cessation of hostilities.

On 19 July, following the failure of their last ground offensive with accompanying heavy losses, the communists had indicated that they were prepared to sign an armistice with the Republic of South Korea, which agreed to this move under considerable pressure from the United States. At this late stage there was a real danger that the communists might still launch an all-out air and ground offensive, perhaps using their Il-28 bombers to strike at bases in Japan, and in that case the war would almost certainly escalate further to include attacks on mainland China. Lists of targets beyond the Yalu had already been drawn up, and there was a stockpile of atomic weapons in Okinawa ready for use by the USAF Strategic Air Command if the need arose.

Meanwhile, the air war went on, the Sabres claiming thirty-two enemy fighters destroyed in the course of July. On the 11th Major John F. Bolt, a US Marine Corps (USMC) pilot flying Sabres with the 51st Wing, shot down his fifth and sixth MiGs to become the only USMC ace of the Korean War; on the 15th James Jabara scored his fifteenth and final victory; and on the 19th and 20th two more 4th Wing pilots, Captain Clyde A. Curtin and Major Stephen L. Bettinger, also became jet aces. Bettinger was in fact the thirty-ninth and last jet ace of the war, but it was several months before his status could be confirmed. After destroying his fifth MiG he was himself shot down and captured, and for fear of reprisals the UN kept his kills secret until he was repatriated in October. One other Sabre was also lost on that day.

At 1700 hours on 22 July, three Sabres of the 51st Wing led by Lt Sam P. Young entered MiG Alley at 35,000 feet on an offensive patrol. Young felt a little depressed; in thirty-four missions he had

not yet fired his guns in anger, and it was beginning to look as though he would never get his chance. On this July afternoon, however, his bad luck broke. Ahead and below, four MiGs swept across his path at right angles. Young dived down, lined up his Sabre carefully, and blew the number four MiG apart with a long burst of fire.

It was the last time that Sabre and MiG met in combat, although not the final Sabre victory. On 27 July 1953, the day fixed for the armistice to come into effect, F-84 Thunderjets of the 49th and 58th Wings made three strikes on airfields in North Korea, while the 4th, 8th and 51st Wings redeployed half their Sabre force to satellite airfields just in case the communists retaliated with a last-minute air attack. About a dozen MiG-15s were sighted by 4th Wing Sabre pilots escorting fighter-bombers on an airfield strike near Chunggangjin, but the enemy fighters sped away across the Yalu and were not seen again.

A few minutes later, however, Captain Ralph S. Parr of the 4th Wing sighted a twin-engined aircraft on an easterly heading and went after it with his wing-man. The aircraft was a twin-engined Ilyushin Il-12 transport, a type not previously encountered in Korea. Whether the pilot had decided to take a short cut across the narrow salient of Korean territory jutting into Manchuria at this point, or whether he was flying supplies to one of the North Korean airfields, will never be known. Parr made two passes and the Il-12 crashed in flames. It was the last communist aircraft to be destroyed in the Korean War, and Captain Parr's tenth victory.

'There is little doubt in my mind,' wrote General Weyland after the armistice, 'that the outcome of the conflict would have been vastly different had enemy domination of the air reversed the military positions of the Communists and the United Nations Command.'

But the enemy never achieved such

domination, although at times they came perilously close to it; and the credit for that, beyond all doubt, belongs to the F-86 Sabre, its pilots and the ground personnel who laboured under often appalling conditions to keep the fighters flying.

Chapter 5
The All-Weather Sabres

I N DECEMBER 1950, the month in which the Sabre made its operational debut over Korea, production of the A model drew to a close with the delivery of the last of 554 aircraft. In the meantime, the basic fighter design had undergone some radical changes as North American set about adapting what was already considered to be a proven combat aircraft in order to meet two separate USAF requirements.

During wartime operations over Germany, the USAAF had learned, the hard way, the bitter lesson that unescorted bombers could not hope to penetrate deeply into enemy territory in daylight without suffering unacceptable losses. Consequently, in 1946 Strategic Air

Command originated a requirement for a so-called 'penetration fighter', primarily to act as an escort for the Convair B-36 bomber. The idea was that such an aircraft, operating from bases in Western Germany and possessing a combat radius that would take it as far as Kiev in the Ukraine, should be capable of sweeping ahead of the bombers and establishing the necessary air superiority en route to the target area.

The Lockheed Aircraft Corporation, McDonnell and North American all put forward proposals. Lockheed's design, the XF-90, was aerodynamically advanced, heavily armed and had the necessary range, but it was seriously underpowered; McDonnell's aircraft, the XF-88, had an

The first prototype North American YF-93A, 48-317. The aircraft was NAA's answer to a USAF requirement for a penetration fighter.

An F-86D Sabre launching a salvo of 2.75-in folding-fin aircraft rockets (FFAR) from its ventral pack. Many initial problems were experienced with this system.

inferior combat radius and operational ceiling.

North American's proposal, originally designated F-86C, was potentially the most promising of the three. It retained the basic Sabre wing, although the span was increased to 38 ft 9 in, and its superbly contoured fuselage was enlarged in cross-section to accommodate an afterburning 6,250 lb thrust centrifugal type Pratt & Whitney XJ48-P-1 turbojet, the available thrust rising to 8,750 lb with reheat. The F-86A nose intake was replaced by NACA flush-type intakes which permitted the installation of AI radar in the front fuselage. The fuselage was stream-contoured to achieve the maximum possible reduction in drag, and twin-wheel main undercarriage units were fitted to support the fighter's 25,500 lb loaded weight.

The F-86C bore little resemblance to its stablemates, and was allocated the new designation of YF-93A. In June 1948, when the USAF placed an order for 118 production F-93A fighters, the aircraft's future seemed assured; but by the time the first of two prototypes (serial 48-317) flew on 25 January 1950, the operational requirement had changed and the penetration fighter idea was shelved.

F-86D: USAF's All-Weather Sabre

However, the second requirement, for a specialized all-weather interceptor, was still very much alive. North American's answer to it, the F-86D, was an aircraft bold in concept. Not only would the traditional interceptor armament of cannon or machine-guns be replaced entirely by air-to-air missiles, but the whole weapons system would be controlled by the pilot alone. Admittedly, the original F-86D design, begun in May 1948, had envisaged a two-seater aircraft, with a second crew member assisting the pilot in making radar-controlled interceptions and being responsible for navigation, but the performance limitations imposed by the installation of a second crew position – coupled with other attendant problems such as restricted fuselage fuel tank space – led to this concept being reconsidered. In the end, it was the availability of improved automated AI radar, reducing the operator's workload, that tipped the scales in favour of the single-seater.

Engineering design work on the single-seat F-86D (NA-164) was begun on 28 March 1949. The USAF showed an immediate interest in the project, and on 7 April work was started on the production version, the NA-165, and North American began building a mock-up on 1 June.

The first of two YF-86D prototypes (50-577 and 50-578) went to Muroc on 28 November 1949 and flew for the first time on 22 December, with George Welch at the controls. Much of the early test flying involved the evaluation of the electronic control system fitted to the afterburning General Electric J47-GE-17. At an early stage in the aircraft's design, it had been realized that pilots would find difficulty in monitoring the engine behaviour, especially during an AI radar intercept requiring the use of afterburner, so to overcome this problem North American and General Electric joined forces to develop a complex engine control system for installation in production F-86Ds. This involved the use of a single throttle lever control which, by means of an electronic fuel selector, determined the amount of fuel being supplied to the engine and afterburner to maintain maximum efficiency even when the throttle was slammed open and shut rapidly. In short, the aim was to correlate the interaction of engine and afterburner automatically. NAA made seventy-four test flights to evaluate this system, and the first batch of engines so modified was available for installation in production airframes late in 1950.

The news that the Soviet Union had detonated a nuclear device infused a sense of urgency into the all-weather interceptor programme, and on 7 October 1949 NAA received a letter contract for 122 production F-86Ds. A formal contract was approved on 2 June 1950, the total on order having meanwhile risen to 153. During this period the aircraft was temporarily re-designated F-95A, as it had little commonality with the original F-86 Sabre, but this was changed to F-86D-1-NA on 24 July 1950. The reason for the change in the first place was all to do with the unit cost of the aircraft; North American felt that, as the F-86D had so little in common with the earlier Sabre, it could justifiably be classed as a new model, and a higher unit price tag be fixed accordingly. The USAF initially agreed, but after further review decided that the aircraft was a logical extension of the F-86 programme and the designation therefore reverted to F-86D.

Both YF-86Ds were flown without the fire control system, which was still under development by the Hughes Aircraft Corporation. The prototype system, the 50-kilowatt E-3, was approved by the Air Materiel Command on 17 February 1950 and was delivered to North American on 26 May; after some changes, it was installed in the second YF-86D (50-578) and tested in September. The test programme was delayed when the YF-86D was damaged at Edwards AFB (as Muroc was now known) as the result of an undercarriage malfunction, resuming on 17 October 1950.

The E-3 fire control system was installed in the first thirty-seven production F-86Ds pending delivery of the more complex 250-kW E-4, but even at this stage delays began to beset the programme. It was not until July 1951 that the first production E-3 system was delivered to NAA, and since aircraft could not be accepted for service without the system, it was October 1952 – three years after the original letter contract – that the USAF took delivery of the last of its thirty-seven F-86D-1s.

The situation with the E-4 system was just as bad, if not worse. The first set was delivered in December 1951, three months behind schedule, and was found to have a power output of only 180 kW instead of the planned 250 kW. The first batch all suffered serious malfunctions, mostly because of extremely poor quality control at the manufacturer's works. Components were wired incorrectly or were of the wrong type, and foreign objects such as screwdrivers were found in the systems' innards. The upshot was that some systems had to be returned to the sub-contractors for repair, and for eleven modifications demanded by the USAF. The first modified E-4 system, installed in F-86D-5 50-492, began its test programme on 13 July 1952. In the meantime, completed F-86D airframes piled up at Inglewood; at one time, in the winter of 1952–3, there were more than 320 F-86Ds awaiting the installation of the E-4 system and other electronic components, including radar, engine controls and autopilots.

Meanwhile, aerodynamic flight testing had revealed a number of problems created by changes of design from the original F-86A. The wing of the F-86D was generally similar to that of the F-86A, except that it was strengthened; the fuselage was dimensionally larger, the vertical tail surfaces were increased in area and a slab-type tailplane adopted for improved longitudinal control. The most noticeable external change was the design of the nose, which now featured a lowered nose intake topped by a 30-inch fibreglass radome housing the antenna of the Hughes AN/APG-36 search radar.

Once the snags had been cured, deliveries of production F-86Ds to Air Defense Command went ahead at a rapid rate. Photograph shows three aircraft in formation over the west coast of America.

All these necessary changes added up to increased drag, and a number of aerodynamic refinements were incorporated in production aircraft. Vortex generators were positioned around the fuselage and tail assembly so as to create a vortex pattern downstream of their location, re-energizing the slow-moving boundary layer airflow and delaying its separation from the surface, thereby reducing drag.

The F-86D's innovative weapons system also produced some teething troubles, all of which contributed to the slippage of the production programme. Early problems with the F-86D's armament, which comprised twenty-four 2.75 inch folding

---

Lt-Col William F. Barnes in the cockpit of the F-86D Sabre in which he set a new world air speed record of 715.697 mph at the Salton Sea, California, on 16 July 1953. The previous record of 698.505 mph, set on 19 November 1952 by Capt J. Slade Nash, was also held by an F-86D.

fin aircraft rockets mounted in a retractable ventral pack, lay in its electronic linkage with the fire control system.

The weapons system was designed to work as follows. On a typical air defence mission beginning with a cold start, the F-86D would be off the ground in about four minutes, which included warming-up time, and would then take eleven minutes to climb to 45,000 feet at full power. The pilot would then initiate the search phase, the AN/APG-36 (AN/APG-37 in later models) radar antenna sweeping an area 68.5 degrees left and right of the centreline in a three-and-a-half second cycle and also, if required, 33.5 degrees up and 13.5 degrees down. When a target was acquired at a range of up to 30 miles the radar locked on to it and the AN/APA-84 computer then worked out a lead collision course, which the pilot followed by keeping the 'blip' on the AI radar scope inside a one-inch circle.

When the automatic tracking system indicated 20 seconds to go, the system instructed the pilot to turn on to a 90-degree collision course, at which point he decided to launch six, twelve or all twenty-four rockets and pressed the trigger switch. The computer controlled the actual firing, extending the rocket pack in half a second and initiating the firing sequence when the target was about 500 yards away. It took only one-fifth of a second to fire the full salvo of twenty-four rockets, each weighing eighteen pounds, the missiles fanning out like a charge of shotgun pellets to make sure of a hit. The rocket pack retracted in just over three seconds, and a symbol on the radar scope, which illuminated at a range of 250 yards, warned the pilot to break off.

Launching a full rocket salvo presented few problems; these tended to arise when the pilot selected a ripple-firing sequence, a procedure that saw frequent malfunctions. The system was updated and refined, but by the time the snags were ironed out the programme had slipped by two years, and it was not until April 1953 that the F-86D

F-86D Sabres of the 406th Fighter Wing, RAF Manston, seen on 12 February 1958. The 406th was deactivated in May.

began to enter service with active Air Defense Command units.

Thereafter, deliveries proceeded rapidly, and by the end of 1953 600 F-86Ds were in service with the Air Defense Command. Eighteen months later, 1,026 – 73 per cent – of the Command's 1,405 interceptors were F-86Ds serving with the US Air Forces overseas; some were assigned to the Fifth Air Force in Korea late in 1953, but the 'Sabre-Dog' was a far heavier fighter than the standard F-86 and it did not take kindly to operations from the still fairly primitive South Korean airfields. It was withdrawn after only a brief period of service in the Far East. F-86Ds did, however, equip the 199th Fighter Interceptor Squadron of the 154th

Fighter Group, Hawaiian Air National Guard, until they were replaced by Convair F-102A Delta Daggers in the early 1960s.

In the continental United States, F-86Ds equipped the following Fighter (All-Weather) Wings and their component squadrons. 1st FW (27th, 71st and 94th FS); 14th (37th, 48th and 49th FS); the 15th and 33rd FW; the 35th FW (39th, 40th and 41st FS); the 40th FW; the 51st FW (16th, 25th and 39th FS); 52nd FW (2nd, 4th and 5th FS); 53rd FW (13th, 14th and 15th FS); 54th FW (42nd, 56th and 57th FS); 84th FW (496th, 497th and 498th FS); 86th FW (525th, 526th and 527th FS); 325th FW (317th, 318th and 319th FS); 326th FW (320th, 321st and 322nd FS); 327th FW (323rd, 324th and

F-86D Sabre of the Hawaii Air Guard.

325th FS); 328th FW (326th, 327th and 329th FS); 329th FW (330th, 331st and 332nd FS); 337th FW (312th and 460th FS); 355th FW (354th and 469th FS). After first-line service, F-86Ds were also allocated to the 111th, 120th, 122nd, 125th, 159th, 173rd, 181st, 185th, 196th and 198th Squadrons of the Air National Guard.

F-86Ds also served in the United Kingdom, equipping the 406th Fighter Wing (512th, 513th and 514th Fighter Interceptor Squadrons) at RAF Manston from November 1953. The 512th FIS moved to Soesterberg in the Netherlands in November 1954, but the rest of the 406th remained at Manston until May 1958, when the Wing was deactivated. By that time, all-weather defence of UK airspace had been taken over by the Gloster Javelin.

Two European-based F-86D units were assigned to Strategic Air Command control in 1958. These were the 497th and 431st Fighter Interceptor Squadrons, which were based at Torrejon and Zaragoza in Spain and which were transferred to SAC from the United States Air Forces in Europe (USAFE) on 5 July 1958 and 1 September 1958 respectively to provide air defence for SAC B-47s which were deployed to Spanish bases on *Reflex Alert* missions. Each squadron had an establishment of twenty-four Sabres. They reverted to USAFE control on 1 July 1960 and re-equipped with the Convair F-102A Delta Dagger shortly afterwards.

Despite the F-86D's many technical innovations, pilot workload remained high; in fact, the 'Sabre-Dog' required more pilot training than any other type in USAF service. An F-86D all-weather school was established at Perrin AFB, Texas, which was equipped with an Erco flight simulator

F-86D of the 406th FW at readiness, RAF Manston, Kent, May 1957.

that duplicated all the functions of the F-86D's cockpit, including attack modes. The 'real thing' was practised by launching the 2.75 inch *Mighty Mouse* rockets at a banner target – a 30 by 6 foot plastic mesh panel fitted with metal discs to produce echoes on the F-86D's AI radar – which was usually towed a mile or so behind a B-45.

All production F-86Ds were fitted with a 15.6 ft diameter ribbon drag chute, beginning with the F-86D-45 variant that entered service in April 1954. This reduced the aircraft's landing roll from 2,550 to 1,600 feet, considerably enhancing the safety factor in all runway conditions.

In all, 2,504 F-86Ds were built for service with the USAF, equipping twenty Air Defense Command Wings at the end of 1955. Meanwhile, considerable strides had been made in speeding up the elapsed time between the detection of a hostile target by the ground radar warning system and passing the relevant information to the interceptor force; the existing system, based on detection and control techniques developed during the Second World War, was no longer adequate in an age of high-speed jets. A major advance was made in 1953 with the USAF's acceptance of SAGE, a semi-automatic ground environment system developed by the Massachusetts Institute of Technology. This was an early datalink system in which all information received from surveillance radars was processed by a high-speed digital computer and transmitted to a receiver installed in the interceptor, where it was converted into factors such as heading,

Many F-86Ds were converted to F-86Ls – one of which is pictured here – with the addition of advanced electronics.

The first production F-86K, 54-1231. North American produced 120 F-86Ks for delivery to friendly foreign air forces.

speed, altitude, target bearing and range. This information was displayed in the cockpit and the interceptor automatically positioned for a lead-collision attack with its E-4 fire control system, eliminating the need for any voice communication.

Early in 1956, beginning with the older aircraft, F-86Ds were progressively withdrawn from the Air Defense Command fleet for overhaul, modification and installation of the necessary datalink equipment. This included an AN/ARR-39 datalink receiver, an AN/ARC-34 command radio (replacing the earlier AN/ARC-27), and an AN/APX-25 Identification Friend/Foe (IFF) transponder. An AN/ARN-31 glide slope receiver was also fitted.

Aircraft so modified were re-designated F-86L, the F-86D-10 to F-86D-40 becoming the F-86L-11 to F-86L-41, while the F-86D-45 to F-86D-60 became the F-86L-45 to F-86L-60. The first F-86L flew in October 1956 and the new model showed few external changes, the most noticeable being that the wingspan was increased to 39.1 feet with the addition of twelve-inch wingtip extensions. Armament and engine were the same as for the F-86D and performance was also similar, although the increased wingspan gave a better turning performance at altitude.

The introduction of the F-86L filled a gap until the F-102A and F-106A interceptors became available, and when this happened the all-weather Sabres were assigned to Air National Guard squadrons, beginning with the 108th (Chicago ANG) FIS in 1957. In all, twenty-three ANG squadrons equipped with the type, the last to use it being the 196th (Ontario, Cal) FIS in 1965.

F-86D Data
Span: 37.12 feet.
Length: 40.26 feet.
Height: 15 feet.
Wing area: 287.9 feet.
Engine: One General Electric J47-GE-17
    or GE-17B rated at 5,400 lb s.t. dry and
    7,800 lb s.t. with reheat.

Weight:
    empty: 13,518 lb.
    maximum: 19,975 lb.
Performance:
    Max speeds:
        sea level 692 mph.
        40,000 feet, 612 mph.
    Max rate of climb at sea level:
        12,150 feet per minute.
    Operational ceiling: 49,750 feet.
    Combat radius: 277 miles.
    Ferry range: 769 miles.

F-86K: NATO's All-Weather Sabre

In the latter half of 1952, at the instigation of the US Air Materiel Command, North American Aviation began investigating the possibility of redesigning the F-86D to produce a simplified all-weather fighter that could be built in Europe and issued to NATO air forces. The original Air Materiel Command requirement called for a two-seater, but North American argued that this would involve much time-consuming structural redesign and so the single-seat layout was retained. Work on the new Sabre variant, designated NA-205 Sabre-K, was begun at Inglewood on 14 May 1953.

The F-86K differed from the Sabre-D mainly in armament and fire control systems, the F-86D's *Mighty Mouse* missile tray being replaced by a battery of four 20 mm M-24A-1 cannon with 132 rounds per gun. The F-86D's complex and troublesome E-4 fire control system was also replaced by the North American MG-4, a simplified system which used the same AN/APG-37 radar antenna but which was considerably more effective, computing a course for lead-pursuit attack and automatically providing the pilot with firing range and break-off time. The movement of the armament forward required an eight-inch extension to the fuselage to preserve the centre of gravity location.

The first of two YF-86K-1-NA prototypes (52-3630 and 52-3804), converted on the assembly line from standard F-86D-20-NA airframes, was flown for the first time on 15

July 1954 by North American test pilot Raymond Morris. In the meantime, an agreement for the licence manufacture of the F-86K had been negotiated with the Societa per Azioni Fiat of Turin and a contract signed on 16 May 1953 for the assembly of an initial batch of fifty aircraft from components built at Inglewood with funds supplied by the Mutual Defence Assistance Pact. The first Fiat-assembled F-86K flew in June 1955.

In order to accelerate deliveries, a contract was placed with North American in December 1953 for the assembly of 120 F-86Ks, all of which were delivered by the end of 1955. Of these, one was retained in the USA for trials work, fifty-nine were delivered to the Netherlands and sixty to Norway. The aircraft equipped Nos 700, 701 and 702 Squadrons of the Royal Netherlands Air Force, and Nos 334, 337 and 339 Squadrons of the Royal Norwegian Air Force.

Of the 221 F-86Ks eventually assembled by Fiat, the last batch of forty-five differed from earlier aircraft in having each wingtip extended by one foot, and being fitted with leading-edge slats. The slats and the increase in wing area considerably improved manoeuvrability, reducing stalling speed from 144 to 124 mph and the take-off run by 800 feet. Overall stability was also improved; an earlier tendency to roll and yaw at low speeds being eliminated. The modifications increased the all-up weight by 850 lb, but this was far outweighed by the improved handling characteristics. All F-86Ks in service with the Royal Netherlands Air Force were retrospectively modified in this way. Sixty-three of the F-86Ks assembled by Fiat were delivered to the Italian Air Force, where they equipped the 21°, 22° and 23° *Gruppi* of the 51ᵃ *Aerobrigata Caccia Ogni Tempo* (All-Weather Fighter Air Brigade); Italy also operated the two YF-86K prototypes, shipped across as pattern aircraft. Of the remainder, eighty-eight went to Federal Germany, equipping the *Luftwaffe's Jagdgeschwader* 74 at Neuburg, and sixty to France's *Armée de l'Air*, equipping the 13ᵉ *Escadre*. Six went to Holland and four to Norway as replacement aircraft.

As a single-seat aircraft the F-86K was far from ideal as an all-weather interceptor, but it filled a dangerous gap in the early 1960s when NATO's European air defences were making the transition from transonic to supersonic combat aircraft. It was not until the late 1950s that the gap began to be plugged with the delivery of the first Convair F-102A Delta Daggers to the all-weather interceptor squadrons of the USAF in Europe; from then on, the F-86Ks formed a second line of all-weather defence behind these formidable aircraft. During the latter part of its operational career, the F-86K's capability was enhanced by the addition of two Sidewinder AAMs to its armament.

F-86K Data

Power for the F-86K was provided by a General Electric J47-GE-17B turbojet, the engine having a military rating of 5,425 lb for thirty minutes and a normal continuous rating of 4,990 lb, boosted by full afterburning to 7,500 lb for fifteen minutes. At a combat weight of 18,379 lb the aircraft was capable of 692 mph at sea level and 612 mph at 40,000 ft. Maximum initial climb rate was 12,000 ft/min, time to 40,000 ft off the runway was 7.3 minutes, and operational ceiling was 49,600 ft. In the area intercept role, the F-86K's combat radius at an average cruising speed of 550 mph was 272 miles, but with two 100-gallon drop tanks the aircraft had a ferry range of 744 miles. Empty weight was 13,367 lb, and loaded weight in the area intercept role 20,171 lb. Dimensions were : span, 37 ft 1½ in; length, 40 ft 11 in; wing area, 287.9 sq ft.

The main F-86K producer was Fiat of Turin, which eventually built 221. Aircraft seen here are from the first batch of fifty, assembled from components manufactured at Inglewood.

Chapter 6
Canada's Sabres

EARLY IN 1949, the Canadian Government decided that the Sabre was the logical choice to form the nucleus of a new Royal Canadian Air Force (RCAF) jet fighter force, and Canadair Ltd of Montreal was selected to build the aircraft under licence. The original contract – for 100 F-86s – was signed in August 1949, and specified that the first aircraft was to be delivered twelve months later. It was the F-86A that featured in the contract, but by the time the first aircraft was complete the North American factory had switched to the production of the much-improved F-86E, so this model was also introduced on the Canadair production line at Cartierville. The sole F-86A completed by Canadair (serial number 191-010) flew on 9 August 1950 and received the RCAF designation Sabre Mk.1; the Canadair-built F-86E was designated Sabre Mk.2.

From the earliest days of the Canadian Sabre programme, much thought had been given to the possibility of replacing the aircraft General Electric J47 engine with the Canadian-designed Orenda turbojet. In 1950 an early 6,000 lb thrust Orenda 1 was installed in a North American-built F-86A airframe, and in October that year flight testing began at Edwards AFB, California, to evaluate the high altitude, high speed characteristics of this combination. This aircraft, designated Sabre Mk.3 by Canadair, was flown by Jacqueline Cochran to a new Women's World Air Speed Record of 652 mph (1,049 km/h) on 18 May 1953; Miss Cochran also became the first woman to fly faster than Mach One on that day.

In 1952, by which time the original Canadian Sabre order had been multiplied many times, some modifications were

A Canadair Sabre Mk 2 shows off its paces in a vertical climb.

The sole F-86A completed by Canadair (191-010) and designated Sabre Mk 1. It flew on 9 August 1950.

made to the aircraft's cabin air conditioning system and its associated cabin layout, and the J47-GE-12 engine was replaced by the 6,100 lb thrust J47-GE-27. The modified aircraft was designated Sabre Mk.4. In the following year the 6,335 lb thrust Orenda 10 turbojet was introduced to the Canadair production line after about 800 Sabres had been built, and at the same time the F-86F's 'six-three' wing leading edge modification was incorporated. Some redesign of the airframe was necessary in order to accommodate the Orenda, which was slightly larger in diameter than the J47. These modifications were fairly straight-forward, and the first Orenda-powered Sabre, designated Mk.5, flew on 30 July 1953. Some 300 Sabre Mk.5s were built, out of a total production so far of 1,100, but the Orenda 10 was really an interim engine and a new model, the Orenda 14, was soon introduced. This featured a two-stage turbine and produced a thrust of 7,600 lb, while weighing about 300 lb less than the

Sabre Mk 2s of No 1 Fighter Wing RCAF (Nos 410, 439 and 441 Sqns) at RAF North Luffenham, 1954.

Sabres of No 410 Squadron, North Luffenham, over the flat landscape of East Anglia.

Orenda 10. Aircraft fitted with the new engine were designated Sabre Mk.6.

The 25 per cent increase in power, coupled with the decrease in weight, had a marked effect on the Sabre Mk.6's climb and high altitude performance. The Mk.6 could climb to 40,000 feet in two-thirds of the time taken by the Mk.5; initial climb rate was 11,800 feet per minute, and operational ceiling a little above 50,000 feet. It could also operate in the ground-attack role, carrying a 4,000 lb underwing load of bombs, rockets or fuel tanks.

On 1 October 1952, 1 Air Division RCAF was formed for overseas service as Canada's air contribution to the North

Sabre Mk 2s of No 441 Sqn RCAF, North Luffenham. Note that the second aircraft has its speed brakes extended.

Sabres of No 2 Fighter Wing, Gros Tenquin, France, taking off during Exercise *Coronet*, August 1953.

Atlantic Treaty Organization (NATO). Ultimately, the division was to exercise operational control of four fighter Wings, each of three squadrons, based in western Europe and equipped with Sabres.

In fact, because of the urgency dictated by events in Korea, and escalating east-west tension, the RCAF contribution began a year earlier with the formation of No 1 Fighter Wing RCAF (NATO) at RAF North Luffenham, Rutland, on 1 November 1951. The Wing's three squadrons, Nos 410, 419 and 441, had all taken part in the air defence of Great Britain during the Second World War, and this was to be their task once more in the face of a new threat. The air defence mission was shared by the F-86A Sabres of the USAF 81st Fighter Wing, which had arrived at RAF Shepherd's Grove and RAF Bentwaters, Suffolk, three months earlier. The Canadians were to remain at North

Luffenham for the next three years, departing for the continent only when the UK air defence role could be assumed adequately by the Sabres and Hunters of RAF Fighter Command.

Meanwhile, as bases in Europe were being made ready to receive them, additional Sabre Wings were forming and working up in Canada. In November 1952 No 2 Fighter Wing's three squadrons – Nos 416, 421 and 430 – left Canada on *Leap Frog 2*, the transatlantic crossing via Greenland, Iceland and the United Kingdom. No 2 Wing became established with forty-eight Sabres at Gros Tenquin, France, and was followed to Europe in March 1953 by No 3 Fighter Wing (Nos 413, 427 and 434 Squadrons) which went to Zweibrücken in Germany. By the end of the year the RCAF fighter complement in western Europe was complete with the deployment of No 4

Canadair Sabre Mk 6 of No 444 Sqn, RCAF, Baden-Söllingen.

Fighter Wing – Nos 417, 422 and 444 Squadrons – to Baden-Söllingen, Germany.

Meanwhile, the end of the war in Korea in the summer of 1953 had made it possible to release sufficient numbers of F-86F Sabres for service with USAF units in other theatres, Europe having the highest priority, and it was decided to equip three Twelfth Air Force Wings with the type during the course of the year: all three had been operating F-84G Thunderjets. The 36th Fighter Wing, at Bitburg, Germany, had been tactically operational since August 1948, soon after the start of the Berlin crisis, and had introduced jet fighters (Lockheed F-80 Shooting Stars) to the post-war continent of Europe; it received its first F-86Fs in May 1953. The other German-based F-84 unit to receive Sabres in 1953 was the 86th Fighter Wing at Landstuhl, later Ramstein; the third unit to re-equip was the 48th Fighter-Bomber Wing at Chaumont, France.

Two more Sabre-equipped units were assigned to the Twelfth Air Force in December 1954: these were the 21st Fighter-Bomber Wing and the 388th Fighter-Bomber Wing, which were equipped with F-86H Sabres and were established respectively at Chambley and Etain-Rouvres Air Bases, France. The 21st FBW, previously assigned to the Ninth Air Force, performed special weapons tactical air operations as part of the NATO air defences in Europe. The USAF Sabres in Europe were mostly replaced by F-100s from 1956.

The US and Canadian Sabre Wings formed part of 4th Allied Tactical Air Force, which was organized very much on a national basis. Its other component was the French 1er Commandement Aérien Tactique (CATAC). In general the Canadian and American Sabre squadrons exercised with one another, although there were occasional squadron deployments to Volkel in Holland and Wildenrath in northern Germany, both in the 2nd ATAF area, when the RCAF pilots had the chance to pit their Sabres against Royal Netherlands Air Force F-84G Thunderjets (which the Canadians referred to rather contemptuously as 'Lead Sleds') and RAF Sabres which equated with their own.

The 4th ATAF Sabre squadrons, like their 2nd ATAF counterparts in the north, took turns at maintaining the NATO *Zulu* alert commitment, which meant keeping a battle

58

flight of two Sabres from each Wing on immediate standby and the remainder at fifteen minutes' readiness. In time of war, the requirement was for the whole fighter force to be airborne within one hour of the alert sounding.

In the summer of 1954, by which time the Canadian squadrons had mostly re-equipped with the Sabre Mk.5, 1 Air Division took part in Exercise *Carte Blanche*, the biggest NATO air defence exercise held up to that time. The Air Division's Sabre squadrons, with a large white X marking on their tails and wingtips, formed part of the 'Southland Air Force' and put up about one-third of the 6,000 sorties flown by 4th ATAF. There were other exercises, but the next biggest after *Carte Blanche* was *Counterpunch*, which was held in September 1957. On this occasion part of the Sabre force was dispersed to pre-stocked airfields in France, from where the aircraft flew air defence, target saturation and armed reconnaissance sorties.

By this time the whole Sabre force of 1 Air Division was equipped with the Sabre Mk.6, and the Sabre Wings on the continent had been reinforced by the redeployment of No 1 Fighter Wing from North Luffenham. No 410 Squadron was relocated at Baden-Söllingen on 14 November 1954, followed by the move of No 441 Squadron to Zweibrücken on 20 December, and on 31 March 1955 No 419 Squadron redeployed to Marville. A few days later, North Luffenham was handed back to the Royal Air Force to become the RAF's Night and All-Weather Conversion Unit.

For the RCAF Sabre pilots, the routine of European flying was broken by regular twice-yearly visits to Rabat, in Morocco, for armament practice. These trips involved a *Leap Frog* type of exercise and two Bristol Freighters were required to go along as support aircraft. APCs in Morocco continued until 1957, when the squadrons began to use the new Armament Practice Range at Decimomannu in Sardinia – a much preferred location, as it involved only a short hop over water.

In 1957, four of 1 Air Division's Sabre squadrons (Nos 410, 413, 416 and 417) were returned to Canada and their places taken by four squadrons (Nos 400, 419, 423 and 440) equipped with Avro Canada CF-100 all-weather fighters. One squadron of these heavyweights, referred to by the Sabre pilots as 'Clunks', was deployed with each fighter wing, No 440 Squadron, for example, joining No 3 Wing at Zweibrücken.

On 2 July 1959, it was announced in Ottawa that the Canadair-built CF-104 Starfighter had been selected to replace the Sabre in the squadrons of 1 Air Division. The competition to provide a Sabre replacement for the RCAF had been keen; aircraft in the running, in addition to the Starfighter, were the Grumman Super Tiger, the Hawker Siddeley Buccaneer, the Dassault Mirage IIIC, the Fiat G.91, the Northrop F-5A and the Republic F-105 Thunderchief. The RCAF's first choice was the F-105, powered by a Canadian-built Orenda Iroquois engine, but the latter was cancelled and the programme proved far too expensive. The Super Tiger had already been rejected by the US Navy (USN), and a version for Canada was no more than a proposal; the Buccaneer did not meet mission requirements and, like the Fiat G.91, lacked the necessary high-speed performance; the Northrop F-5A had not then flown, and the Mirage III at that time lacked adequate strike/reconnaissance capability. So the choice fell on the F-104.

In 1961 the Sabre replacement question was becoming urgent, because the Mk.6 was suffering from a growing number of fatigue problems – so much so that in March that year 1 Air Division banned all air fighting manoeuvres with the type, which meant that it was virtually restricted to armed reconnaissance and ground attack. In December 1961, No 427 Squadron was notified that it was to disband in the following August, but that it would reform as 1 Air Division's first CF-104 unit.

Re-equipment of all the RCAF Sabre squadrons was well under way early in

Sabre Mk 6 of No 427 'Lion' Squadron RCAF, No 3 Wing, Zweibrücken.

1963, accompanied by a reshuffle of units following the closure of Gros Tenquin during the year and the disbandment of No 2 Wing. No 1 Wing remained in France at Marville with Nos 439 and 441 Squadrons; No 3 Wing continued to be based at Zweibrücken with Nos 427, 430 and 434 Squadrons; and No 4 Wing was at Baden-Söllingen with Nos 421, 422 and 444 Squadrons, Nos 421 and 430 Squadrons having been re-assigned to the other wings from Gros Tenquin. The last RCAF Sabres in Europe were retired on 14 November 1963, when No 439 Squadron at Marville was stood down.

The squadrons of 1 Air Division now had the demanding new role of low-level strike and reconnaissance. Since the CF-104 had a tactical nuclear capability, it was also a task that carried an awesome burden of responsibility. There were many pilots who would remember the relatively carefree, dogfighting Sabre days with great affection.

Chapter 7
Sabres for Britain

IN THE spring of 1952, it was agreed that the Royal Air Force would receive nearly 400 Canadian-built Sabres under the Mutual Defence Assistance Pact. The majority of these, as a matter of priority, were to be assigned to the fighter squadrons of the 2nd Tactical Air Force in Germany, then equipped with the de Havilland Vampire FB.5; others were to equip one air defence Wing of RAF Fighter Command in the United Kingdom, replacing an aircraft which had already shown itself to be totally unsuited to the air superiority role in Korea – the Gloster Meteor F.8. The Sabre was seen essentially as a stop-gap aircraft until the Hawker Hunter became available, but although this type had been allocated super-priority production status it would be at least 1954 before the home-based squadrons of Fighter Command began to re-equip with it, and even longer before it reached the front line in Germany. The whole Sabre delivery was to be completed by December 1953.

Because of the prohibitive cost of dismantling and reassembling the aircraft, on top of dock and shipping expenses and the time that would have been lost, delivery by sea was ruled out. It was decided to fly the Sabres over the Atlantic in convoys, the operation being given the name *Becher's Brook* and drawing on the experience gained during *Leap Frog*, the operation in which two RCAF Sabre Wings were flown to Europe beginning in the summer of 1952.

Three RAF pilots accompanied the first *Leap Frog* movement as observers; on the second, three pilots of No 1 Overseas Ferry Unit, including its CO, Sqn Ldr T. Stevenson AFC, flew in convoy with the

Canadians to acquaint themselves with the route and its problems. Ferrying was to be under RCAF operational control, with the use of USAF airfields en route and American administrative support and rescue facilities.

Operation *Becher's Brook* began on 8 December 1952, when the first convoy of twelve Sabres left for the UK from Bagotville, an RCAF airfield beside the Saguenay River in Quebec Province. Their flight brought to light many problems associated with the Arctic weather, which the RAF had not fully appreciated, and as a result Sqn Ldr Stevenson recommended a more specialized set-up, with more emphasis on IFR (Instrument Flight Rules) formation flying and on instrument let-down technique using the radio compass.

In January 1953, between the first and second convoys, the Overseas Ferry Unit changed its name to No 1 Long-Range Ferry Unit, and on 1 February it was renumbered No 147 Squadron and moved to RAF Benson in Oxfordshire. It was completely reorganized to meet the growing and more specialized commitment. Servicing staff were divided into two mobile parties, each joining one of two Hastings support aircraft so that they could be positioned at each stop along the route ahead of the convoy.

The RAF ferry pilots received conversion training on the F-86E Sabre with No 1 Fighter Wing RCAF at North Luffenham, Leicestershire, before joining the squadron in Canada, where they underwent a further training period in extreme cold and bad weather, the kind of flying conditions they might expect over the North Atlantic, and also in Arctic survival.

Whenever possible, *Becher's Brook, Leap*

Frog and USAF Sabre movements to Europe were synchronized. Weather forecasts, airfield, radio and navigational information were passed by teleprinter some hours before take-off of each flight and pilots were briefed accordingly. Flight plans were drawn up and crews waited on 'standby', swaddled in Arctic flying clothing that comprised string vests, Long Johns, sea boots, stockings and sweaters under a rubberized fabric waterproof suit.

The recognized procedure was to start up in sections of four and to move off at five-minute intervals. Each section took off in pairs then joined up in close formation for the climb to cruising altitude, which was usually 35,000 feet. Often, formations entered cloud soon after take-off and stayed in it for 30,000 feet before levelling out on top. Climb and cruise were regulated to comply with flight plan speeds. At the top of the climb the practice was for the leader to tune into the Ocean Weather Ship beacon for homing – it was positioned on track – and for Nos 2 and 4 to tune to the rescue aircraft frequency. In this way an accurate check was kept on the flight plan and fuel states, flight intervals were maintained and pilots were able to arrive at the destination airfield on time to complete a radio compass let-down, under Instrument Flight Rules (IFR) if necessary, in perfect safety. In good weather, a gradual descent would be made on track.

One of the problems encountered during the operation was aileron control locking, caused by the contraction of the aileron torque tubes in the intense cold at 35,000 feet. As a matter of course, landings were made without the use of ailerons. On one occasion, water in a circuit breaker caused an electrical short and a Sabre's drop tanks fell off. Luckily the aircraft was on the ground at the time, waiting to take-off. In freezing conditions, the ground crew worked magnificently and replaced the tanks in less than an hour; the usual time to assemble drop tanks was three hours, under normal conditions.

During the early movements, No 147 Squadron began the ferry run from Bagotville and flew via Goose Bay in Labrador, across the North Atlantic to Bluie West One (Narsarssuak) in southern Greenland, Keflavik in Iceland, and Prestwick, Ayrshire before dispersal to maintenance units in the UK. Later movements started from St Hubert, just outside Montreal, and terminated in the UK at Kinloss in Morayshire. For one short period, the arrival airfield was Royal Navy Air Station (RNAS) Lossiemouth. The whole flight covered a distance of some 3,000 miles, and the average airborne time for the crossing was six and a half hours.

In all, No 147 Squadron flew ten Sabre convoys across the Atlantic. They varied from the smallest of eleven aircraft to the biggest single movement of fifty-four. The last convoy landed in Scotland on 19 December 1953, a year to the day after the arrival of the first aircraft. Crossing times could be anything from four days to three weeks, depending on the weather. On two occasions, to clear an accumulation of waiting Sabres, a double-shuttle system was used; sixty-four aircraft were ferried by thirty-two pilots, the crews returning in the support Hastings of Nos 24 and 47 Squadrons for a second Sabre on the completion of each leg.

The first three Sabres of the 430 that eventually crossed the Atlantic for RAF service were designated Mk 2s; these went to form the Ferry Conversion Unit under the control of No 1 RCAF Wing at North Luffenham. The remainder were all Mk 4s, which had a modified cabin air conditioning system and other minor modifications.

Five Sabres were lost during the actual ferry operation. They were XB534, which crashed three miles south-east of Prestwick on its delivery flight on 19.12.52; XB610 which dived into the ground after instrument failure seven miles north-east of Grantown-on-Spey, Morayshire, on 5.4.53; XB863, which suffered electrical failure in cloud and crashed six miles north-east of St Felix de Valois, Canada, on

Sabre Mk 4 XB603 of the Sabre Conversion Flight, RAF Wildenrath. This aircraft was written-off on 15 June 1953 when it lost power on an overshoot.

5.6.53; XB882, lost after the ejection seat fired when the cockpit canopy opened near Broughty Ferry, Angus, on 18.7.53; and XB925, which crashed near Kinloss on 28.9.53.

Some RAF Sabres were allocated to No 229 Operational Conversion Unit at RAF Chivenor, Devon, to provide fast jet experience for squadron pilots. A few were sent to the Central Gunnery School, the Fighter Weapons School and the Air Fighting Development Squadron. The first operational unit to re-equip with the aircraft was No 3 Squadron at RAF Wildenrath, Germany, which gave up its Vampire FB.5s in May 1953 and moved to Geilenkirchen in July. No 67 Squadron, also at Wildenrath, equipped with Sabres at the end of May 1953 and remained there alongside the Vampire FB.5s on No 71 Squadron, which also converted to Sabres in October. A Sabre Conversion Flight at Wildenrath supplemented No 229 OCU's output of pilots by providing familiarization for Vampire pilots.

By the end of 1953, eight RAF squadrons within 2nd Allied Tactical Air Force were equipped with the Sabre Mk.4. In addition to the Wildenrath Wing, comprising Nos 67 and 71 Squadrons, these were No 4 Squadron at Jever, Nos 20, 26 and 234 Squadrons at Oldenburg, No 130 Squadron at Brüggen, and of course No 3 Squadron at Geilenkirchen, which had the task of proving the aircraft under operational conditions, formulating tactical manoeuvres and so on. Two more squadrons, No 93 at Oldenburg and No 112 at Brüggen, equipped with the Sabre early in 1954.

Once they had got used to characteristics such as the Sabre's higher landing speed, pilots found conversion straightforward. There were no drastic changes from previous types; engines still flamed out, aircraft still sometimes went out of control, electronics still failed from time to time. In the Sabre Pilot's Notes, though, one section – rectification action to be taken in the event of equipment failure – caused a few raised eyebrows: a surprising number of failures carried the single word 'eject'.

Engine failures and sudden losses of power were not uncommon. On 15 July 1953, XB603 of the Sabre Conversion Flight suddenly lost power on an overshoot and crash-landed, the aircraft being damaged beyond repair. Three months later, on 17 September, XB683 of No 67 Squadron went into a spin six miles south of Liège, Belgium, again as a result of engine trouble, and was abandoned by its pilot. On 16 November, the same squadron suffered a tragic accident when two of its Sabres, XB690 and XB730, collided in formation near München-Gladbach. The latter aircraft exploded, killing its pilot; the other pilot ejected.

These were the only RAF Sabre losses of 1953, which in view of the intensity of flying was not a bad record. In the mid-1950s the main threat was still expected to come from bombers attacking at high level, and a great deal of emphasis was consequently placed on practice combat at high altitude. This involved one-v-one, two-v-one, two-v-two and two-v-four combats between Sabres and, occasionally, between Sabres and Venoms, which in 1953–4 were beginning to equip two RAF Wings in 2nd ATAF. The de Havilland Venom FB.1 had excellent manoeuvrability at high altitude and could almost always out-turn the Sabre, but was inferior in performance on every other count. However, there was little of operational value to be derived from encounters between Sabres and Venoms.

Sabre Mk 4s of No 112 Sqn, 2 ATAF, Brüggen. The Squadron's characteristic shark's teeth marking was first adopted on its Kittyhawks in the Western Desert during WWII.

As one Sabre pilot put it:

'The only way to derive a valid performance comparison of this kind would be to set up an encounter meticulously beforehand, and to conduct it in such a way as to bring out the precise parameters in question, minimizing others which could otherwise skew the results but which, in this particular exercise would be incidentals. That never happened. I was based at Jever; the Venoms were over at Fassberg 100 miles further east. Our encounters were infrequent and purely by chance, the result perhaps of trailing our coat across the sky in their direction when we had nothing better to do. The odds were against a formation of Venoms being airborne at the same time, in the same area, and at altitude, as they were in the ground-attack role. That kind of air combat may be fun, and good training in formation flying, lookout, manoeuvring and tracking, but without the very rigid controls mentioned above the comparative outcomes are meaningless. Even ciné results are meaningless; the chap who brings back a good steady shot of you may himself have been recorded on your own camera five minutes before. Who knows? It boils down always to: "I shot you down – No, I shot you first".I think it was not until the later introduction of instrumented Air Combat Manoeuvring Ranges with telemetry that we could really boil this down to hard conclusions. And there, it is the people in the control cabin on the ground who have the true story, not the participants.'It may be true that a Venom could out-turn a Sabre; so too could a Tiger Moth. For a variety of reasons I would still choose to be in the Sabre. In air combat you don't play to the other fellow's strengths but you try to induce him to play to yours. If, for real, you found yourself at a disadvantage, and if the performance of your aircraft allowed (as it did in the Sabre), you would disengage if you had any sense and try again if you could. But in a mock encounter where nobody is shooting, you tend not to do that. You stay in the mêlée until a low fuel state dictates that you go home. After all, you were looking for a dogfight, you've found one – in which everyone remains unscathed and in play throughout – so why leave? But to translate any lessons from this into real terms would be unreliable and quite unrealistic.'

Like their Canadian counterparts in the south, the 2nd ATAF Sabre pilots paid regular visits to an armament practice camp, although in the RAF's case such visits were made to the Weapons Training Unit in the unglamorous surroundings of the island of Sylt. There were also exchange visits with other NATO air forces, the Sabre pilots having the opportunity to 'mix it' with F-84 Thunderjets of the Netherlands, Belgian and Danish Air Forces, and with Ouragans of the *Armée de l'Air*.

The rigorous training was not without its cost; the RAF lost twenty-three German-based Sabres in 1954, and about half the accidents were due to aircraft or systems failure. February was a particularly black month; on the 10th, XB681 of No 3 Squadron ran into the overshoot area and the pilot raised the undercarriage in order to stop, resulting in the aircraft being damaged beyond repair, and on the 24th the same squadron suffered a double tragedy when XB643 and XB667 flew into the ground as a result of faulty information passed during GCA training at Henri-Chapelle, Belgium. On the same day, XB866 of No 26 Squadron vanished after radar contact was lost in cloud over the north German coast; neither it nor its pilot were seen again.

Engine problems led to two accidents in March 1954. In the first, on 3 March, XB912 of No 112 Squadron suddenly lost power during an overshoot and made a forced landing near Brüggen; the second happened on the following day, when XB936 of No 67 Squadron failed to become airborne and crashed off the end of the runway at Wildenrath. In a third accident, on 22 March, XB600 of No 67 Squadron was abandoned after suffering a total electrical failure. June 1954 was again a bad month, with four Sabres lost; XB648 of No 130 Squadron swung on take-off at Brüggen on 3 June and its nosewheel retracted, the aircraft being damaged beyond repair; the pilot of No 112 Squadron's XB884 was forced to abandon the aircraft after the controls failed on the approach to Brüggen on the 16th; XB940 of No 4 Squadron force-landed short of fuel on the autobahn eight miles east of Hamburg on the 22nd, and XB818 of No 234 Squadron crashed near Jülich after suffering engine failure on the 29th. On 8 July, XB647 of No 4 Squadron stalled on an overshoot and dived into the ground three miles from the end of the Jever runway, and on the 23rd XB865 of No 26 Squadron became overstressed during air combat manoeuvres, caught fire and was abandoned near Hede.

The only Sabre loss in August 1954 involved XB638 of No 20 Squadron, which hit a tree on the approach to Oldenburg and dived into the ground on the 5th, but September and October were costly, with nine aircraft lost through various causes. The run of trouble started on 2 September, when XB734 of No 26 Squadron crash-landed at Oldenburg after its undercarriage jammed in the 'up' position. Five days later, XB627 of No 67 Squadron ran out of fuel and crashed near Peer, Belgium, and on 22 September XB899 of No 20 Squadron suffered an undercarriage failure and force-landed at Schleswigland.

On 8 October, XB937 of No 4 Squadron dived into the sea during armament practice off Sylt, and later in the month five Sabres were lost during a bleak ten-day period starting on the 19th, when XB988 of No 130 Squadron caught fire on a night navigation exercise and crashed seven miles north-east of Kassel. On the 26th, XB628 and XB729 of No 71 Squadron were

abandoned following a mid-air collision ten miles north-west of Krefeld; three days later, XB927 of No 130 Squadron crash-landed in the undershoot area after an engine failure on the approach, and XB860 of No 234 Squadron broke up in the air over Wintraal in the Netherlands. The latter accident led to the grounding of all 2nd ATAF Sabres for some weeks for structural checks, the process being carried out in rotation by the Sabre Wings so that at least part of the force remained operational, but flying operations did not return to their previous level until early in the new year.

The first three months of 1955 were relatively trouble-free; only three Sabres were lost, and two of the accidents were attributed to weather conditions. On 4 February, XB760 of No 71 Squadron dived into the ground near Jülich after the pilot lost control in cloud, and on the 24th XB623 of No 26 Squadron apparently hit a patch of ice on the runway at Oldenburg and skidded off the runway into a snowbank, which was hard enough to damage the aircraft beyond repair. Earlier, on 10 February, No 26 Squadron had lost another Sabre when XB839 dived into the ground eight miles south-west of Oldenburg; the cause of this accident was never established.

There was an unfortunate and tragic accident on 5 April, when XB634 of No 67 Squadron collided with Avro Anson TX238 on the approach to Wildenrath, leaving no survivors from either aircraft. On 3 May, XB616, flown by the Geilenkirchen Wing leader, suffered an engine failure and made a forced landing near Pfaffendorf, and on the 16th XB699 of No 3 Squadron dived into the ground near Lontzen, Netherlands. No 3 Squadron lost a second aircraft on 16 June, when XB633 sank back on take-off and crash-landed in the overshoot area.

In April 1954 the first Hawker Hunter F.4s arrived in Germany and were allocated to Nos 98 and 118 Squadrons, both of which had been operating Venoms. The two newly-equipped squadrons moved to

Sabre Mk 4 XB629 leading two aircraft that succeeded it in Germany: a Hawker Hunter F.4 of No 112 Sqn (note the shark's teeth) and a Supermarine Swift FR.5 of No 4 Sqn. XB629 served with Nos 112, 93 and 3 Sqns, and was stricken off charge in December 1958.

Jever, where they operated alongside the Sabres of Nos 4 and 93 Squadrons to form a four-unit air defence wing. In May, No 14 Squadron also exchanged its Venoms for Hunters at Fassberg and moved to Oldenburg to form a three-squadron air defence wing with the Sabres of Nos 20 and 26 Squadrons, and in June the latter became the first Sabre squadron to convert to the Hunter, followed by No 4 Squadron at Jever in July and No 20 Squadron in November.

There were further Sabre losses during the year. On 5 July, XB950 of No 112 Squadron dived into the ground near Heerlen, Netherlands, after its engine caught fire; on the 12th, XB932 of No 130 Squadron flew into the undershoot area at Brüggen; and on the 15th, also at Brüggen, XB880 of No 71 Squadron lost height on the approach, hit the ground and exploded.

The third day of August saw the loss of XB548, one of the original batch of Sabres to be delivered. Flown by a No 93 Squadron pilot, it flew into the ground while recovering from a dive at Meppen Ranges, Germany. On 16 August this accident was repeated when XB808 of No 20 Squadron also hit the ground at Meppen. August's third accident occurred over the United Kingdom when XB700 of No 26 Squadron collided with Sea Hawk WM964 near Yeovilton on the 17th. On 2 September, XB735 of No 234 Squadron, on deployment to Italy, suffered an engine failure while approaching to land at Brindisi; the aircraft broke up. Engine failure on the approach also resulted in the loss of XB822 of No 93 Squadron at Jever on 1 October.

Early in 1956 conversion to the Hunter F.4 gathered momentum. Nos 67 and 93 Squadrons, respectively at Brüggen and Jever, relinquished their Sabres in January, and the Brüggen Wing became an all-Hunter force with the conversion of Nos 112 and 130 Squadrons in April. No 71

Squadron at Wildenrath also received Hunters during the month. The last two squadrons to convert were Nos 3 and 234 at Geilenkirchen, in May 1956.

Now that the Hunter had sounded the retreat for 2nd ATAF's Sabres, it fell to the pilots of No 147 Squadron to collect them from their bases and fly them to the airfields of various civilian contractors who were to refurbish them for service with other NATO and friendly-foreign air forces. As a first step, the aircraft were flown to RAF Benson, Oxfordshire, where they were serviced before going on to their ultimate destinations. The last Sabre out of Germany was XB670 of No 3 Squadron, which was ferried to Benson by Master Pilot S. Fell on 21 June 1956. In all, 267 Sabres were flown back from Germany and, after overhaul, were transferred to USAF control.

While the Sabre held the line in Europe, two RAF squadrons assigned to UK air defence were also equipped with the type. These were Nos 66 and 92 Squadrons at RAF Linton-on-Ouse, Yorkshire, a base they shared with the Gloster Meteor NF.11 (later NF.14) night-fighters of No 264 Squadron. No 66 Squadron was the first to exchange its Meteor F.8s for Sabre Mk.4s, in December 1953, and No 92 Squadron followed suit in February 1954. The two squadrons received an allocation of sixty aircraft, providing them with 100 per cent reserves, and of these, eighteen were lost in accidents during the two years or so the type remained in service. Engine flameouts or sudden power loss resulted in the loss of seven aircraft (XD710, XD722, XD729, XD768, XD771, XD772 and XD773), one aircraft – XD712 of No 66 Squadron – broke up while recovering from a dive and crashed into the sea off Scunthorpe on 16 June 1955, two (XD755 and XD780) crashed as a result of stalls on the landing approach, another two (XD 758 and XD 776) were abandoned after their pilots received fire warning indications, and XD713 suffered irreparable damage when its pilot raised the undercarriage to stop following a tyre

burst. Two aircraft of No 66 Squadron, XD711 and XD716, were lost in a mid-air collision over the Yorkshire Wolds north-west of Hornsea on 16 June 1954, both pilots ejecting successfully, and the remaining three were destroyed through hitting high ground. On 22 July 1954, XD707 and XD730, both of No 66 Squadron, flew into high ground in cloud at Kinder Scout, Derbyshire, and on 22 September that year high ground near Easingwold, Yorkshire, claimed XD733 of No 92 Squadron, out on a night navigation exercise.

Both squadrons used the Sabre until the spring of 1956, when they re-equipped with Hunter F.4s. Most of the UK-based Sabres, like their 2nd ATAF counterparts, were transferred to the USAF for later overseas disposal, although one aircraft – XB982, formerly with No 92 Squadron – was allocated to Bristol Siddeley for trials work and flew until 1959, fitted with an Orpheus 12 engine. It was scrapped in June 1962.

The last RAF Sabre to leave RAF Benson was XB617, also an ex-No 3 Squadron aircraft, which was flown to Speke, Liverpool by Sergeant M. Lackman to be handed over to Airwork Ltd, the company which had been responsible for the storage, servicing and modification of RAF and RCAF Sabres throughout the aircraft's operational service in NATO. The principal F-86 spares depot was at Langar, Nottinghamshire, where No 30 Air Materiel Base had been set up by the RCAF in 1952; this was controlled by 1 Air Division at Metz and was made up of Base HQ and four different sections. The largest of these was the 312th Supply Depot, whose seven and a half acres of warehousing space held 80,000 different items. Langar was also responsible for technical liaison with Airwork teams working with operational Sabre Wings in NATO. Major airframe and engine overhaul work was undertaken by the Bristol Aeroplane Company Ltd at Filton, Bristol.

It was Squadron Leader L.B. Foskett, AFC, Officer Commanding No 147 Squadron when the Sabre was retired from RAF service, who expressed a fitting epitaph for the aircraft.

'As the characteristic whine of the aircraft that had endeared itself to so many of us died away from Benson for the last time, we thought of the host of RAF pilots who had flown this magnificent aircraft during its brief stay in our Service. There can be few who did not gain by the experience. Some, we remember with regret, paid with their lives for that experience. Those of us who gained our first knowledge of swept wings and power controls on the Sabre will not quickly forget it. Neither will the ground staff of 147 Squadron who serviced the first and the last of the RAF's Sabres.'

Chapter 8
Flying the Sabre Mk 4

'RARELY HAS there been an aircraft which so belies its appearance as the Sabre. Despite its advanced aerodynamic lines and its hydraulic and electrical complexity, it is one of the most viceless, most exhilarating aeroplanes one could have the pleasure of flying. It can be said, in fact, that the Sabre is a sheep in wolf's clothing.'

So wrote Flight Lieutenant N.F. Harrison, DSO, one of the pilots who put the Sabre Mk 4 through its paces at the Royal Air Force Flying College's Handling Squadron at Manby, Lincolnshire. The following is Flt Lt Harrison's report on the aircraft's characteristics.

Before describing the handling characteristics it would be as well to cover some of the more interesting technical features of which the Sabre has a profusion. The engine, which gives 5,200 lb static thrust, is a General Electric J47-13, an axial flow design developing its maximum thrust at about 7,900 rpm. The fuel system differs from the British one in that there is no HP or LP cock as such, these controls being incorporated in the throttle and engine master switch respectively. In addition, the fuel pump and flow-regulating part of the system is duplicated so that, should the main fuel pump or any other part of the main system fail, the separate emergency system can be switched on and a re-light made if the engine has stopped.

The internal fuel is carried in five separate tanks. Their total contents are shown on a single gauge, which is calibrated in terms of pounds weight.

This system, though initially strange, soon becomes familiar, and has the advantage that it automatically takes care of specific gravity variations. Thus, when the tanks are full of fuel having a SG of .8, the gauge reading will be greater than when a fuel of SG .76 is used; the range is accordingly increased. A switch labelled *densitometer* is used to cut out the weight-measuring properties of the gauge and enables the volume of fuel to be checked so that it is possible to tell whether the tanks are full before starting up.

In addition to the fuel gauge a flowmeter is fitted. It is very useful when flying for range or endurance; the instrument shows the rate of fuel flow in pounds of fuel per hour, the take-off figure being about 6,000 lb per hour. The flowmeter dial also incorporates a veeder counter type of meter called the *totalizer* which shows the amount of fuel remaining and which can be used as an additional means of checking. The *totalizer* is reset manually each time the aircraft is refuelled. But it is not as accurate as the main fuel gauge which should always be regarded as the master for fuel checks.

The flying controls are perhaps the most interesting feature of the Sabre. The 'flying tail' and ailerons are moved solely by hydraulic power, the rudder alone being operated through the conventional cable system. To cope comfortably with the large changes in fore and aft trim encountered at the highest obtainable Mach numbers, it was necessary to use a more powerful control in the Sabre than the

conventional elevator, which at these speeds shows a regrettable tendency to 'throw in the towel'.

The solution is found in the 'flying tail'. This is a method of controlling the fore and aft attitude by changing the incidence of the tailplane, the elevator being linked to the tailplane in such a way that it moves in its normal sense. Forward movement of the control column operates an hydraulic jack which raises the leading edge of the tailplane (hinged about its rear spar). At the same time the elevator, through its linkage, moves down to assist the action of the more powerful surface. The overall effect of the 'flying tail' is to give the pilot a means of control far more powerful and effective at all speeds, than the elevators alone could provide.

The Sabre's ailerons are noteworthy because of their unusually large area for a fighter aircraft. These big control surfaces would be practically immovable at high speeds were it not for hydraulic operation; the very high rate of roll that can be attained is due entirely to the powered ailerons. Because ailerons and tailplane are power-operated they have no natural aerodynamic self-centering properties and are, in fact, irreversible which means too, that there is no natural 'feel' in the controls.

An artificial feel system is used to serve the dual purpose of giving the pilot 'feel' and centering the control column after it has been displaced from neutral. 'Artificial' is the operative word as the feel remains the same at all speeds, even when the aircraft is on the ground! The system is designed so that the force required to move the control column increases the further it is displaced from neutral; it is completely independent of airspeed. Therefore, it is as easy to apply full elevator at the stall as it is at 600 knots – a fact that is worth remembering as the days of controllable wingless aircraft are not yet with us.

In case of failure of the normal hydraulic flying control system, a standby system comes into operation automatically and an indicator light comes on to show that the standby system is operating. Should automatic selection of the standby system not take place there are two other methods of engaging it. The chances of failure of the normal hydraulic system – excluding those caused by enemy action – are no more likely than with a conventional system. In any case there is always the standby.

Unusual and interesting is the electrically-operated trimming system. The controls consist of a thumb-operated switch on top of the control column. Fore and aft movement of this switch controls nose-down and nose-up movements; sideways movements control lateral level. The rudder trim switch is on the port console.

The only indicator for the trimmers is a single light on the instrument panel. To set neutral fore and aft trim for take-off the thumb switch is moved fore or aft until the indicator light glows to show that the neutral position has been reached after which the switch is released and the light goes out. The same procedure is used to set the lateral and directional trims and the same light glows in each case. In case of failure of the thumb switch, there are standby switches next to the rudder trim switch.

So much, then, for the general description of the Sabre. I shall mention other points of interest as they arise. Meanwhile let us away to the aeroplane.

After completing the pre-flight check and getting into the cockpit a number of differences between British and American practice are immediately apparent. First, the instrument panel. It seems to be filled with a variety of instruments of various sizes and shapes, which have been crowded in apparently

to fill every last square inch of space. But after half an hour or so the arrangement becomes familiar and after three or four hours' flying there is no difficulty at all; it has been said that the longer one flies the Sabre the fewer the number of instruments there seem to be.

On the port side of the cockpit there is a formidable array of switches and a battery of circuit breakers. These switches control cockpit heating and pressurizing, standby trimming and the switches for manually engaging and disengaging the standby flying control system. The starboard side has a further collection of circuit breakers and the controls for engine starting, cockpit lighting, radio and radio compass.

Below the instrument panel there is a panel containing the controls for the armament and the radar-controlled gunsight; there is also a switch which can be used to select a standby inverter should the normal inverter for the flying instruments fail.

There is plenty of room in the cockpit and the view in all directions through the large canopy is excellent. There is nothing of the mild claustrophobia encountered in the cramped cockpits of some fighter aircraft.

Unlike the Martin Baker type, the North American ejector seat with which the Sabre is fitted has no canvas blind to protect the face; operation of the seat is controlled by a small handgrip on the end of each arm rest. Oxygen, 'G' suit, and radio connexions are disconnected automatically as the seat leaves the aircraft.

Until the technique of starting the engine becomes familiar it is a rather tricky business to say the least, as a badly managed start can be the cause of an engine change. Unlike the British systems in which all fuel control is done automatically, this American system requires the pilot to control the entire start with the throttle. The throttle quadrant has a gate at the idling position. When the throttle is pushed outwards it can be moved still further aft into a section which is used to obtain the low fuel necessary for starting. Movement to the fully aft position closes the HP cock. It is to this position that the throttle is moved to stop the engine.

Before starting, an external power source must be plugged in, then the engine master switch on the forward starboard console is switched on. To engage the starter the battery starter switch is moved briefly to 'starter'. This energizes the starter, which will cut out automatically when the engine is accelerating properly. The throttle is then carefully and slowly opened about ¾ inch until the fuel flowmeter is reading about 700 lb/hour and at the same time the throttle is pressed outboard to energize the igniter plugs. The fuel flow is maintained at this figure until the light-up occurs, after which the throttle is kept stationary until the jet pipe temperature settles down. Then the throttle is moved carefully to just past the gate of the idling position, keeping the j.p.t at about 600°C.

Any sudden or coarse movement of the throttle will cause severe over-fuelling, putting the needle of the j.p.t gauge well over the limiting temperature and, in extreme cases, against the stop. Any ten starts that exceed a temperature of 870°C require an engine change and any one start that reaches 1,000°C requires the same drastic treatment. You can thus appreciate that Sabre starting is an operation requiring careful management of the throttle; all movements should be small and made cautiously if one is the sort who shuns embarrassing situations and the glare of publicity.

When the engine is idling at the normal r.p.m. of about 40 per cent (the r.p.m. gauge is calibrated in percentages of the actual engine speed) the flying controls are tested, both normal and standby systems being selected in turn. The operating pressures are checked and control surface movements noted visually. After checking the rest of the cockpit the chocks are waved away and parking brake released.

Nosewheel steering is engaged by pressing a button on the control column and holding it in this position during the period of taxying. The Sabre is a delight to taxi, the foot brakes are smooth and powerful, and the response and control of the steering mechanism is all that could be asked for. On arrival at the run-way, parking brakes are put on and take-off checks made.

The check list is covered by the usual TAFIOHH mnemonic and consists of:

T Trim – All neutral.
A Airbrakes – In; selector to neutral.
F Fuel – Contents, operation of
  flowmeter and totalizer.
I Instruments – Operation. Inverter
  switch to normal.
O Oxygen – Check operation.
H Harness – Locked and tight.
H Hood – Closed.

The harness, by the way, does not have to be locked before take-off because a device is built-in which automatically pulls the straps back and locks them whenever a deceleration greater than 2 to 3 G is experienced.

The aircraft is then taxied onto the runway, lined up, brakes applied, throttle opened and the emergency fuel system tested and exercised. At the end of this test the throttle will be fully open and the take-off can be started merely by releasing the brakes.

The Sabre is guided down the runway using the brakes to keep straight (*not* the steerable nose wheel, which was not designed for use at high speeds) until rudder control is obtained at about 50–60 knots. Initial acceleration is fairly slow; at about 95 knots a steady

backward pull raises the nosewheel, and with a continued backward pull you are unstuck at about 115–120 knots in a pronounced nose-up attitude which is a bit disconcerting at first.

Wheels and flaps are raised and the emergency fuel system switched off. This last point is very important indeed, as should it be forgotten, a rapid opening of the throttle at some other stage of the flight can easily result in flame extinction. Flaps and wheels must be tucked away by the time you reach 185 knots, but as acceleration at this stage is not excessive there is ample time.

To reach climbing speed as quickly as possible the engine is left at full power keeping a careful eye on the j.p.t. which is at, or nearly at, its maximum figure of 690°C. The starting speed for climbing the aircraft clean is 430 knots – high compared with most service aircraft – and it takes some little time to reach this speed. Once it has been attained, how-ever, and the nose raised, the rate of climb indicator starts to read and settles down at about 7,000 feet per minute.

First and strongest impression the Sabre gave us after the first few minutes of flight was that the flying controls were absolutely first-class. Ailerons and tailplane are crisp and powerful, the ailerons being particularly praise-worthy in that they are finger-light and very sensitive. The response from the Sabre's ailerons is as good as could be desired; any quick movement of the control column results in an immediate rolling motion that seems to reach its maximum speed without any preliminary accelerating period; in fact the aeroplane is virtually jolted into the roll. The tailplane is not quite as brisk in its responses (perhaps it's just as well) but at high speeds it is still lighter and far more powerful than any cable operated system and it is a control that must be used with care as very little force is required to obtain large G loads.

It is, in fact, too light for comfort. At low speeds, unless the trimmer is used, stick forces can be high.

After climbing to about 10,000 feet the stall can be checked. Speed is lost by throttling back and opening the airbrakes, which are effective even down to speeds as low as 100 knots. As the speed falls off and the aircraft is kept at a constant height the attitude becomes more and more nose-up until at the stall itself, the nose is some distance above the horizon – a characteristic common to all swept or delta-wing aircraft.

The controls retain their normal feel at all times and there is no stall warning other than a slight buffeting beginning some 5–10 knots before the stall and increasing a little when the stall occurs. The nose drops gently at the stall; there is no wing drop. If the control column is held fully back a fore and aft rocking motion begins with the nose rising and falling alternately, the buffeting increasing as the nose rises and decreasing as it drops. At all times full aileron control is present and, for one's amusement, it is possible to make a stalled descent including turns in either direction. The rate of descent, however, is high and experiments of this kind should not be continued below about 6,000 feet.

Recovery from the stall is straightforward. With flaps and undercarriage down the stalling speed is about ten knots lower, but otherwise the aircraft's behaviour is exactly the same as in the clean condition. Stalling speed for the clean aircraft is about 105–110 knots; for the 'all-down' case, about 90–95 knots. The exact speed varies with atmospheric conditions and the skill of the pilot, as small amounts of G make quite a big difference.

At low speeds, stalling under G results in the nose dropping. Continued backward movement of the control column may cause a wing to drop slightly, but this is always controllable and at the same time pitching begins as in the normal stall.

At high speeds and G loads the Sabre becomes unstable in that it suddenly starts to tighten up and increases the G load automatically, possibly beyond the limit unless it is checked quickly. This feature of the Sabre is its sole bad habit,

and except for this flaw in its behaviour it can be flown to its limits with every confidence.

Having looked at the low speed end of the scale the climb can be resumed and height gained for some high Mach number flying. During the climb it becomes apparent that there is no need to adjust the throttle to restrain the r.p.m. – unlike most British jet engines; but as the higher altitudes are reached the j.p.t. might start creeping past the limit in which case, of course, power must be reduced. The climb performance falls off noticeably after about 30,000 feet, but as there is no point in going very high the aircraft can be levelled off at, say, 38,000 feet to start the dive.

After a general check, the Sabre can be pushed at full throttle into a dive of

about 30 degrees. The speed and Mach number rise rapidly. Nothing happens until about .94M–.95M when either wing starts to get heavy, but this can easily be held with a small aileron movement. The wing heavying tendency may transfer to the opposite wing after a second or so, but at no time does it become worrying. By the time .97M is reached this period is passed and no further lateral unsteadiness is encountered. In a 30-degree dive the aircraft will not accelerate much past .97M and to reach supersonic speed the aircraft must be clean, the dive must be started from at least 35,000 feet and must be vertical, with the throttle fully open.

A dive of this sort is accomplished without approaching any of the aircraft's limits; during the whole performance the IAS remains well within the limiting speed of 600 knots. The only strain is that imposed upon the pilot's nervous system because, for the average cautious man it takes considerable determination and mental effort to half roll, pull through to a vertical dive at full power, and then deliberately to hold the aircraft in this unnatural attitude while the speed builds up.

The wing-heavy period shows up as a few sharp wing drops that occur and disappear almost before they can be corrected, after which nothing more happens except for a nose-up change of trim which is easily held and which can be trimmed out by blipping the trimmer, taking care not to over-control as all controls are very sensitive at these speeds. There is no indication that Mach one has been exceeded, the Machmeter itself may not read more than .98M–.99M, but once its needle has slowed down and eventually stopped, there is no point in pressing on as this movement represents the Mach number terminal velocity. The Sabre, in other words, can only just reach supersonic speed with its present engine.

Recovery can be made either by throttling back and using the airbrakes or simply by pulling out of the dive. The latter method uses up more sky but is quite straightforward; level flight being resumed somewhere around, or a little below, the 20,000 foot mark. There is one point that must be watched when opening the airbrakes, which incidentally are operated by a thumb switch on top of the throttle lever. The airbrakes are set so that on opening they cause a nose-up change of trim. This change is fairly strong at high indicated airspeeds and so must be anticipated and checked if necessary. Just for interest, the rate of descent at 30,000 feet is somewhere between 50,000 and 60,000 feet per minute, and even though you are at a fairly high altitude you are uncomfortably aware of the fact that objects below are getting bigger noticeably faster. And as the TAS is somewhere around 700 knots the racket set up by the airflow is appalling.

Aerobatics and spinning are simple. The sensitive and powerful controls make any manoeuvre effortless and enable a high degree of precision to be maintained. A maximum rate roll done at, say, 400 knots results in the roll being completed almost before the control column is fully over, and, if it is held over, the Sabre rotates through three or four rolls so quickly that, on centralizing, the horizon rolls and pitches crazily for some seconds before one's equilibrium is restored. The rate of roll is about as much as could be used comfortably and approaches the physiological limit.

Loops are easy. The starting speed is 350 knots but the artificial feel causes some unusual stick forces compared with those encountered in a conventional control system. When the loop is started the stick force to get between 3G and 4G is very light and as the loop progresses an increasingly greater stick force is required until, as the Sabre flies round the top of the loop at about 150 knots, a considerable pull is required.

The powerful ailerons make rolls off the top child's play. Even if the speed has fallen to near the stall there is always enough life in them to roll precisely back to level flight.

Spinning is easily checked. From a straight stall the control column is moved fully back and full rudder pushed on firmly and held. The first half turn may be almost inverted but the attitude quickly becomes normal and the Sabre settles down into a slow spin with the nose fairly well down but steadily rising and falling. There is little or no buffeting and the whole affair is very smooth. Some spins, especially to the left, may not develop fully and take the form of a stalled spiral dive. To recover, the normal movements are made and the spin stops within about half a turn, with the control column at about the central position or slightly further forward. There is no limitation on the number of turns that can be made but a four-turn spin, begun at about 18,000 feet, uses up roughly 8,000–9,000 feet of altitude.

Dives to high indicated airspeeds require only a shallow dive and the 'never exceed' speed of 600 knots is reached quickly. There is little impression of speed, even at low altitudes, and it is not until the Sabre's shadow is seen streaking over objects on the ground that you realize just how rapidly distance is being covered.

The elevators are very sensitive at these high indicated airspeeds. If the air is at all bumpy, and until you are familiar with the aircraft, it is best to let the Sabre ride through these rather than attempt to correct for small displacements because of the possibility of over-correcting and setting up a rapid porpoising motion in an attempt to chase the movement. If this occurs it is best dealt with either by leaving it alone or applying a slight back pressure. The

zoom climb of the Sabre is very good and a pull up from ground level at these speeds realizes a good 23,000 feet. During this time, for the sacrifice of 2,000–3,000 feet, an uncountable and dizzy number of upward rolls can be made.

The strong nose-up trim change, which opening the airbrakes at maximum speed causes, will if unchecked result in a 3G pull-out. This is not uncomfortable but must be allowed for if the brakes are extended while G is being applied. There is a school of thought that argues against the practice of 'building-in' a nose-up change of trim, preferring a straight decelerating effect; indeed the nose-up change could, in some circumstances, become an embarrassment.

The circuit and landing is easy and straightforward, the only unusual point being the marked nose-up attitude during the final approach when the speed drops below about 140 knots. At light and medium weights the across-the-hedge speed is 115 knots and the aircraft touches down at about 110 knots. It is easy to scrape the tail on the runway during the roundout, therefore stalled, or nearly stalled, landings should not be made. The brakes are good and a 2,000-yard runway is ample for the Sabre, even in no-wind conditions. The landing is made with the airbrakes open for they give considerable drag even at low speeds.

The Sabre is a very pleasant aeroplane indeed and although its high-altitude performance is not all it ought to be, its good qualities are so numerous that whoever flies it will become an enthusiast. From the flying controls viewpoint the Sabre is a curtain raiser for the coming breed of very high performance aircraft; it would be gilding the lily to ask for better control qualities. The only talking point is the touchiness of the elevator at high speeds but this is a function of the artificial feel system rather than the controls themselves, which retain their response and power at all heights, speeds and Mach numbers. The lesson best taught by this aircraft is that power-operated controls are essential on high-speed aircraft – gone are the days of two-handed pushes and pulls and struggling with surfaces that are only just effective and in some cases completely ineffective.

Chapter 9
Other NATO Air Forces – Sabre Day Fighters

Germany

In the mid-1950s, one of the key policies of Allied Air Forces Central Europe (AAFCE) involved the early re-equipment of the Federal German *Luftwaffe* with modern combat types as part of an expansion scheme that would eventually lead to the full integration of newly-formed German units into the Allied Tactical Air Forces. This in turn would enable air units from other Allied air forces, principally Great Britain and the United States, to be withdrawn. Once again, it was the Canadair-built Sabre that was selected to fill the crucial air superiority gap on NATO's Central Front, and in 1957 seventy-five Sabre Mk 5s were delivered to the *Luftwaffe*. These went to *Waffenschule* 10 at Oldenburg for operational training and were followed by 150 Sabre Mk 6s, with which the *Luftwaffe* formed its first day fighter wing, *Jagdgeschwader* 71 (JG71), at

Ahlhorn. Later, JG71 moved to Wittmundhafen. On 21 April 1961, in continuation of a tradition dating from before the Second World War, JG71 was granted the name *Richthofen*.

Two more Sabre 6 *Geschwader*, JG72 at Leck and JG73 at Pferdsfeld, were also formed. These three units continued to operate in the air superiority role during the early 1960s, while *Luftwaffe* fighter-bomber wings which had been using the Republic F-84F Thunderstreak re-equipped with the Lockheed F-104G Starfighter. In 1964 JG71 also equipped with this type at Wittmundhafen, and the other two Sabre 6 units converted to the Fiat G.91R, assuming a new ground-attack role.

Greece

In 1957, as part of a modernization and expansion programme, 107 Canadair F-86E Sabre Mk 2 aircraft were delivered to the

Canadair Sabre Mk 6 of the *Luftwaffe*'s *Waffenschule* 10, Oldenburg.

Looking extremely sorry for itself, this former *Luftwaffe*, JG71 *Richthofen* Sabre Mk 6 now rests in the air museum at Duxford.

Royal Hellenic Air Force to form a day interceptor component. These equipped the 337, 341 and 343 *Mire* (squadrons) of the 111 *Pterix Mahis* (combat wing), the RHAF's other combat units being equipped with the F-84G Thunderjet at that time. The Sabre units were based at Tenagra and Nia Ankhialos and formed part of the NATO-assigned 28th Tactical Air Command. Conversion to the Northrop F-5A/B began in 1965, but the process was delayed when deliveries were suspended for political reasons in 1967 and was not completed until 1969.

In August 1958, the 341 *Mira* formed an aerobatic team, the *Hellenic Flame*, with five F-86E Sabre 2s, later increased to seven aircraft. The previous team, the *Skyblazers*, had been run by the 337 *Mira* and comprised four F-84G Thunderjets. The *Hellenic Flame* carried out displays in West Germany, Italy, Turkey and France before disbanding in September 1964.

Italy

The *Aeronautica Militare* was the principal recipient of refurbished ex-RAF Canadair Sabre Mk 4s, 188 of which were delivered in 1956–7 to equip the 4ª *Aerobrigata*. This comprised the 9° *Gruppo* at Grosseto, the 12° *Gruppo* at Gioia del Colle and the 10° *Gruppo* at Grazzanise. It was not NATO-

Canadair CL-13A Sabre 19392 of the Greek Air Force aerobatic team, *Hellenic Flame*, seen in 1962.

assigned, unlike four other Air Brigades equipped with F-84Gs, although it would have come under NATO control in the event of an emergency.

In 1956 the 4ª *Aerobrigata* formed the Italian Air Force's first Sabre aerobatic team, the *Cavalline Rampante* (Rampant Horses) at Pratica del Mare, and this operated with four aircraft for two seasons. In 1957–59 the post was filled by the F-84Fs of the 6ª *Aerobrigata* and also, in 1958–59, by six Sabre 4s of the 2ª *Aerobrigata* at Cameri, whose two *Gruppi* had equipped with the F-86 in the day interceptor role. This aerobatic team was named the *Lanceri Neri* (Black Lancers). The most famous Italian aerobatic team of all, however, was the *Frecce Tricolori*, which formed early in 1961 with nine Sabre 4s and used them until the early months of 1964, when the team converted to the Fiat G.91.

By this time the Canadair Sabre had been phased out of first-line Italian Air Force service. The 2ª *Aerobrigata*'s two *Gruppi*, the 13° and 14°, re-equipped with the Fiat G.91R, while two *Gruppi* of the 4ª *Aerobrigata*, the 9° and 10°, converted to the F-104G Starfighter. The 12° *Gruppo* exchanged its F-86Es for the all-weather F-86K, which it continued to use for some time.

Norway

The Royal Norwegian Air Force (RNorAF) received 115 F-86F Sabres, deliveries starting in 1957. This gave the RNorAF a dual interceptor/strike capability; previously, within the framework of Allied Air Forces Northern Europe, the emphasis had been almost entirely on tactical strike with F-84G Thunderjets, with the exception of two squadrons equipped with all-weather F-86Ks.

The first RNorAF squadrons to equip with the F-86F in 1957 were Skv.331 and Skv.332 at Bodo, near the Arctic Circle, and by mid-1960 the last F-84Gs had been phased out with the conversion of Skv.338 at Orlandet. The F-86F also equipped Skv.336 at Rygge. Conversion to the F-86F

Portuguese Air Force Sabre F-86F of *Esquadra* 51, Rota. Fifty F-86Fs were acquired by Portugal, and the type served until 1959.

entailed some reorganization, three of the day fighter units being paired with an F-86K all-weather squadron; the third F-86K unit was Skv.334.

In the early 1960s, as the first stage of a RNorAF re-equipment programme, Norway was assigned two squadrons of F-104G Starfighters to provide supersonic intercept capability, and in the autumn of 1963 Skv.331 exchanged its Sabres for the new type. In the event, this was the only squadron to receive the Starfighter, as the RNorAF decided that most of the tasks assigned to the F-104 could be filled adequately by a less expensive aircraft. The type chosen was the Northrop F-5A, the first examples of which went to Skv.336 at

Rygge in 1966. Before the end of 1967 a second Rygge F-86F unit, Skv.332, had also begun conversion to the Northrop aircraft, and the F-86F was finally phased out of the inventory in the following year with the conversion of Skv.338 at Orlandet.

It was Skv.332 that provided the Royal Norwegian Air Force's jet aerobatic team, exchanging its Thunderjets for Sabres in May 1957. In 1963, the team – the *Flying Jokers* – replaced its F-86Fs with F-86Ks, and used them until it was disbanded in the autumn of the following year. The *Flying Jokers* was not a permanently-established aerobatic team, being activated whenever aircraft could be spared from operational duties.

Canadair Sabre Mk 2 of the Turkish Air Force at Merzifon AB.

Portugal

The Portuguese Air Force received fifty F-86F Sabres, deliveries starting in 1958, and the first of two squadrons to use the aircraft, *Esquadra* 51, achieved operational status on the type at *Basa Aerea* BA2, Rota, in the summer of 1959. A second unit, *Esquadra* 52, became operational in October at a newly-activated airfield, BA5 at Monte Real, the two squadrons combining to form *Grupo de Caça* 501. The Sabres were responsible for the air defence of the whole of Portugal, their operations controlled by an Intercept Control and Communications Centre at Monsanto. The Sabres were still in service in 1979, the fifteen surviving aircraft amalgamated into the single unit – *Esquadra* 201 – still based at Monte Real.

A Turkish AF Sabre Mk 2 stands alongside other former first-line types – F-84Ds, F-100 and F-102 – in the Air Force Museum.

Some of the latter-day Sabres were ex-Norwegian aircraft. By 1980 the F-86Fs had been placed in storage, leaving the Portuguese Air Force without an interceptor element, a gap that was only partially filled by the acquisition of ex-*Luftwaffe* Fiat G.91s armed with Sidewinder AAMs.

Turkey

Deliveries of eighty-two Canadair Sabre Mks 2 and 4 to the Turkish Air Force began in 1954, the aircraft equipping a three-squadron day interceptor wing at Merzifon Air Base. Some F-86Es were also delivered from the North American production line to make up for attrition. The three Sabre squadrons were responsible for air defence as part of the Turkish Air Force's 2nd Tactical Air Force. Fifty F-86D Sabres were also supplied in 1959, equipping two all-weather air defence squadrons. The Sabre day fighter wing remained operational until 1967, when Turkey's 2nd Tactical Air Force disbanded, and in the following year the F-86Ds were also withdrawn, their all-weather role being taken over by the Convair F-102 Delta Dagger from 1969. The F-86Ds were ex-Royal Netherlands Air Force aircraft.

Chapter 10
Australia's Sabres

IN OCTOBER, 1951 – by which time the F-86 had already established itself as a combat-proven design in the skies over Korea – the Australian government decided to obtain a manufacturing licence for the Sabre, albeit in much-modified form. Although the basic F-86 possessed the range capability required by the RAAF, it was demonstrably underpowered and its machine-gun armament left much to be desired. The Australians therefore decided to replace the F-86E's J47-GE-27 engine with a 7,500 lb thrust Rolls-Royce Avon RA.7 turbojet, developed for the Hawker Hunter fighter, and to install two 30 mm Aden cannon in place of the six 0.50 machine-guns.

The decision to use the RA.7 engine – which in due course was named the Avon – led to some airframe design changes. The British engine was fatter and shorter than its American predecessor and weighed some 400 lb less, so it had to be positioned further aft in the fuselage in order to preserve the original centre of gravity. This in turn meant that the engine was no longer supported entirely by the forward fuselage, so the rear fuselage was shortened by 26 in and the forward fuselage lengthened by a corresponding amount. In this way the original fuselage length was retained. Also, the greater power of the Avon engine made it necessary to increase the size of the air intake, and this was achieved by splitting the front fuselage horizontally and lowering the bottom line three and a half inches. This enabled the intake to be enlarged without having to make extensive changes to the cockpit area. The rear fuselage, however, had to be completely redesigned to support the Avon's jet pipe in such a way that neither tailplane inertia

loads nor tail unit flight loads were transferred to the engine. When all the modifications had been made, only about forty per cent of the original F-86F fuselage structure was retained.

Licence manufacture of the Sabre was undertaken by the Commonwealth Aircraft Corporation Pty (CAC), the aircraft being allocated the Company designation CA-26 and the RAAF designation Sabre Mk 30. The prototype Avon-powered Sabre (A94-101) flew for the first time on 3 August 1953, and a few days later Flt Lt Bill Scott of the RAAF was loaned to Commonwealth Aircraft to carry out the initial flight test programme. Few snags were encountered during flight testing – in fact, the only trouble encountered with the prototype was a minor centre of gravity problem which was solved by weighting the nose with 80 lb of lead ballast and, in the production model, by moving forward a pump supplying emergency power to the controls – and the aircraft soon showed some remarkable performance characteristics, manoeuvring easily at altitudes in excess of 50,000 feet and registering an initial climb rate of 12,000 ft/min, nearly twice that of the F-86E.

The first production Sabre Mk 30, designated CA-27, flew on 13 July 1954 and was handed over to the RAAF on 30 August. The initial batch of twenty-two Sabre Mk 30s were powered by imported Rolls-Royce Avon engines; subsequent aircraft were fitted with the CAC-built Avon Mk 20, which had a constant-taper Solar jet pipe. The first twelve Mk 30s were allocated to the newly-formed Sabre Conversion Flight of No 2(F) Operational Training Unit at Williamtown, New South Wales.

Sabre Mk 32s of the Butterworth Wing join an RAF Victor B.1, Canberras and Javelins in a flypast during the period of the confrontation with Indonesia in the early 1960s.

The Avon 20-powered Sabres, of which twenty were built, were designated Sabre Mk 31, and the earlier batch was later modified to this standard. They were followed by sixty-nine Sabre Mk 32s, which were fitted with the F-86F's '6-3' wing leading edge, uprated Avon Mk 26 engines and four hardpoints for underwing stores.

The Avon Sabre equipped the RAAF's three permanent fighter units, Nos 3, 75 and 77 Squadrons. On 11 November 1958 No 3 Squadron was deployed to Butterworth, Malaya, as part of the Commonwealth Strategic Reserve, and was joined there by No 77 Squadron on 1 February 1959, the two Sabre squadrons forming No 78 RAAF Wing together with the Canberras of No 2 Squadron. By this time the offensive support role of the Commonwealth Air Forces in the campaign against the communist terrorists in Malaya was virtually over, and no air strikes at all took place in the first seven months of 1959. In August, however, several terrorist camps east of Bentong in Northern Pahang were spotted by Auster reconnaissance aircraft, and, as no ground forces were available in the area, a formation of Sabres from Butterworth was called in to strafe pinpoint targets marked from the air.

With the end of the Malayan Emergency the RAAF Sabre squadrons assumed their primary role of air defence, a task they shared with the Javelins of No 60 Squadron RAF and, to a lesser extent, the Hunters of

A RAAF Sabre Mk 32 rolls away from the camera aircraft to demonstrate its Sidewinder AAM installation.

No 20 Squadron RAF. The air defence task assumed new importance during the period of confrontation between Malaysia and Indonesia in the early 1960s, especially when armed Indonesian regular troops began to make incursions into the Malay peninsula in September 1964. As an insurance against possible attacks on Commonwealth bases on Singapore Island and the RAAF base at Butterworth, HQ Far East Air Forces called all its strike/attack units to alert status, and on 28 October 1964 the RAAF Sabres took part in a full scale air defence exercise.

With the end of Confrontation in 1966 No 78 RAAF Wing provided detachments of Sabres to Labuan Island, off the coast of Sarawak, to relieve the Hunters of No 20 Squadron which had provided air support for ground forces operating along Malaysia's disputed Borneo frontier with Indonesia. The RAAF Sabres' air defence capability had now been enhanced for some time by the addition of a pair of Sidewinder air-to-air missiles, mounted on the inboard underwing stores pylons. Missiles for the two Malaysian-based squadrons had been flown direct from the USA in two C-130A Hercules aircraft of No 36 Squadron RAAF during February 1960, the Sidewinder installation having been tested and approved on Sabre A94-946 in the previous year.

On 1 June 1962 a fourth Sabre Mk 32 unit was added to the RAAF Order of Battle. This was No 79 Squadron, which had disbanded at Morotai in November 1945 after flying Spitfires in WW II. It now

CA-27 Sabre Mk 31 A94-915 of the RAAF aerobatic team, the *Marksmen*, drawn from No 2 OCU in 1968. The trim is black and yellow. Note the smoke-generating pipe along the fuselage.

reformed at Singapore and, supported by the C-130As of No 36 Squadron, flew to Ubon in Thailand as part of a South-East Asia Treaty Organization (SEATO) deployment on the same day. It remained there until August 1968, when it redeployed to Butterworth. It disbanded in July 1968.

Meanwhile, the decision had been taken to replace the Sabre with the Dassault Mirage IIIO(A). The first squadron to re-equip, early in 1964, was No 75 at Williamtown, and in May 1967 it took its Mirages to Butterworth to replace No 3 Squadron, which had returned to Williamtown in February for re-equipment with the French fighter. No 3 Squadron in turn went back to Butterworth in February 1969 to replace No 77 Squadron, which returned to Williamtown to receive its complement of Mirages.

Chapter 11
Non-NATO Sabre Customers

Argentina

In 1961, the Argentine Air Force received 30 F-86F Sabres, refurbished by North American, to replace the elderly Gloster Meteor Mk 8 aircraft which had formed the backbone of its interceptor/strike force since 1948. The Sabres were assigned to *Grupo 6 de Caza* (6th Fighter Group) and remained in service until late 1979 when, reduced to about 20 in number, they began to be replaced by the Israeli Aircraft Industries Dagger.

Bolivia

The Bolivian Air Force purchased nine F-86F Sabres from Venezuela in 1973, and these equipped the 1° *Grupo Aereo de Caza* at Santa Cruz. The four survivors were still on the inventory at the end of 1992, although thought to be no longer airworthy.

Chile

Twenty-five refurbished F-86F Sabres were supplied to Chile in the early 1960s, and these equipped *Grupo 8* at Antofagasta in the north of the country, forming the Chilean Air Force's primary air defence unit. From 1974, the Sabres were replaced by Northrop F-5Es.

China (Nationalist)

The Chinese Nationalist Air Force (CNAF), based on the island of Taiwan, received some 250 F-86F Sabres, which equipped the 1st, 2nd and 3rd Fighter Wings from 1957. During the Formosa Crisis of 1958, con-

A Vulcan B.1 (XH502) of No 617 Sqn RAF makes an impressive background to a pair of Chinese Nationalist Air Force F-86Fs as it takes off from their Taiwan base. The Vulcan was on a goodwill tour of the Far East.

90

siderable publicity was given to the use of the Sidewinder AAM by CNAF Sabres in action against Chinese Communist MiG-17s. The crisis, which began in August with the shelling of Nationalist-held islands in the Formosa Strait, lasted until October and there were frequent air battles between the opposing sides, the Nationalist Sabres claiming the destruction of thirty-one MiGs for the loss of only two of their own number. In fact, only six Sidewinders were launched throughout the conflict, and these destroyed four MiG-17s. The F-86F remained in first-line service with the CNAF until the mid-1970s, when the type was replaced by the Northrop F-5E.

Ethiopia

In 1960, the Ethiopian Government entered into a Mutual Assistance Agreement with the United States and received a batch of twelve F-86F Sabres, plus some North American T-28A advanced trainers. Eleven of the Sabres were still on the Order of Battle in the summer of 1977, when Ethiopia became involved in war with neighbouring Somalia over the disputed Ogaden Desert region, but it is doubtful whether they were used operationally, the Ethiopian Air Force having by that time begun to re-equip with Soviet-supplied types such as the MiG-21. The US type that was used operationally in the conflict was the Northrop F-5A.

Indonesia

In 1972, Indonesia received twelve ex-RAAF Commonwealth Sabre Mk 32s, which formed a single day fighter squadron based at Surabaya. Withdrawal of these began in 1980 when the squadron – No 14 – received its first eight Northrop F-5Es.

Iran

In 1966, 90 ex-*Luftwaffe* Canadair Sabre Mk 6s were delivered to Iran, ostensibly to form a day fighter wing, but in reality this was part of a clandestine arms deal involving Pakistan. The Sabres were sent to Pakistan 'for overhaul' and never returned, being used to make good attrition in the Pakistan Air Force's F-86F Sabre fleet.

Japan

The Japanese Air Self-Defense Force (JASDF) was one of the biggest overseas Sabre customers, with nineteen first-line

F-86F Sabre of No 6 Sqn, Japanese Air Self-Defense Force.

F-86F Sabre 92-7931 of the JASDF's *Blue Impulse* aerobatic team pictured at Tsuiki Air Base in 1973.

F-86F Sabre 02-7988 of the JASDF's HQ Squadron at Iruma.

RF-86F 62-6428 of the JASDF's 501st Reconnaissance Squadron, Iruma.

squadrons using either the F-86F or F-86D. The first five of an initial batch of twenty-two pilots – all of them veterans with WWII combat experience – left for the United States in August 1955 to undergo conversion to the F-86F, having received jet training in Japan on the Lockheed T-33A, and in December the first Sabres arrived in Japan under the Mutual Defense Assistance Programme. These aircraft formed the nucleus of the 1st Squadron, 1st Fighter Wing, which was essentially a training unit, at Hamamatsu. The first eight

Sabres were F-86F-25s, and these were followed by twenty F-86F-30s.

From the outset, the Sabre had been envisaged as forming the backbone of the JASDF, and a licence and joint production agreement was reached between Mitsubishi and North American for the F-86F-40 model. While the necessary facilities were being set up, the initial batch of F-86F-40s was shipped to Japan from the USA in 1956, and by the middle of the following year 180 had been delivered. At that time the JASDF did not possess a sufficient number of qualified Sabre pilots, so forty-five of the North American-built F-86F-40s were placed in storage and eventually returned to the USA in February 1959.

The American-supplied F-86Fs were used to form the JASDF's first tactical jet fighter unit, the 2nd Fighter Wing (Day), which was activated at Chitose in October 1956. This unit comprised the 103rd, 201st and 203rd Squadrons. Exactly a year later the 3rd Fighter Wing (Day) – 101st, 102nd and 105th Squadrons – was activated at Matsushima, and the 4th Fighter Wing (Day), consisting of the 5th and 7th Squadrons, was activated at Matsushima early in 1958.

In April 1958, F-86F Sabres of the 2nd Fighter Wing were scrambled on an actual intercept mission for the first time, and the 3rd and 4th Wings achieved full alert status in the following year. All JASDF Sabre units were under the operational control of the US Fifth Air Force, which was charged with the defence of Japan, Okinawa and Iwo Jima.

The first of 300 Mitsubishi-assembled F-86F-40s flew on 9 August 1956, and the last aircraft was delivered on 25 February 1961. Other units to equip with the aircraft were the JASDF GHQ Squadron at Iruma, the 6th Fighter Wing (4th and 205th Squadrons) at Komatsu, the 7th Fighter Wing (206th and 207th Squadrons) at Hyakuri, all forming part of the Central Command; the 5th Fighter Wing (202nd and 204th Squadrons) at Nyutabaru, the 8th Fighter Wing (6th and 10th Squadrons) at Tsuiki, and the 82nd Squadron at Iwakuni, forming part of Western Command; and the 501st Squadron of Reconnaissance Command at Iruma, which was equipped with RF-86Fs.

Meanwhile, in 1957, the JASDF had received four F-86D Sabres to train pilots for the nucleus of an all-weather fighter force. These were followed, over the next three years, by 110 similar aircraft, most of which went to replace the F-86Fs of the 3rd Fighter Wing, which then moved to Komaki. The 103rd Squadron of the 2nd

Fighter Wing also re-equipped with the F-86D.

On 1 October 1964, the 202nd Squadron of the 5th Fighter Wing became operational with the Mitsubishi-assembled Lockheed F-104J Starfighter, and by the spring of 1966 six more former F-86F units – the 201st, 203rd, 204th, 205th, 206th and 207th Squadrons – had also re-equipped with this type. At this time, 310 F-86Fs, ninety-eight F-86Ds and eighteen RF-86Fs were still on the Order of Battle. Ten years later, by which time the F-104Js that had replaced the Sabre in the first-line squadrons were themselves being replaced by the F-4EJ Phantom, 185 F-86F Sabres were still operational in the combat training role with the 6th, 8th and GHQ Squadrons; they were eventually retired in 1979.

Republic of Korea

The RoK Air Force operated two Wings (Nos 10 and 11) of Sidewinder-armed F-86Fs in the fighter-ground attack role, and one Wing (No 12) of all-weather F-86D interceptors. The aircraft were withdrawn in the late 1970s.

Malaysia

In 1969, the Royal Malaysian Air Force received ten refurbished ex-RAAF Sabre Mk 32s; this initial delivery was followed by seven more aircraft in 1971, the seventeen Sabres equipping Nos 11 'Cobra' and 12 'Tiger' squadrons at Butterworth. The Sabres remained in first-line service until 1978, when they were replaced by the Northrop F-5E.

Pakistan – See Chapter Twelve

Peru

The Peruvian Air Force received one squadron of twelve F-86F Sabres in 1956, and this formed part of *Grupo* 12 at Las Palmas alongside a squadron of Hawker Hunter F. Mk 52s and one of Lockheed F-80Cs. The Sabres (and the Hunters) remained operational until the late 1970s, when they were replaced by the Sukhoi Su-22 Fitter-C.

Philippines

The Philippine Air Force (PAF) was an early recipient of US military aid in the Pacific area of operations, three squadrons of the 5th Fighter Wing equipping with F-86F Sabres in 1957. The Wing comprised the 6th, 7th and 9th Tactical Fighter Squadrons (TFS). In 1977–8 the Sabres were replaced in the 6th and 7th TFS by the Northrop F-5A and the LTV F-8H Crusader; the 9th TFS had earlier converted to a training role. The PAF also operated one squadron of F-86Ds.

Saudi Arabia

Sixteen F-86F Sabres, supported by ten Lockheed T-33A trainers, were delivered in 1958 to form the Royal Saudi Air Force's (RSAF) first combat squadron. In reality they provided little more than a token capability, lacking armament and being frequently grounded through lack of spares and inadequate overhaul facilities. In 1963 the Sabres were sent to Federal Germany to be completely overhauled, returning to service with the RSAF's No 5 Squadron in 1964 with a complete weapons fit. They proved completely incapable of opposing the frequent incursions by Egyptian aircraft, and in 1966 the RSAF received a new air defence system based on a mixed force of Hawker Hunters and BAC Lightnings. Nevertheless, eight more F-86Fs were obtained in 1968, and all aircraft of this type were concentrated in No 7 Squadron. Based at Khamis Muchayt and supported by attached Pakistan AF personnel, the Sabres saw action against fortified Yemeni positions on the border in December 1969, together with Lightnings operating in the ground-attack role, and with the end of the conflict in January 1970 they were returned to Dhahran, where No

Sabre Mk 6 372 of No 1 Sqn, SAAF, taken at Pietersberg during the station's open day in January 1976.

7 Sqn formed part of the fighter OCU. Standards of maintenance were poor, and four Sabres were lost in accidents during 1969–70. In the mid-1970s the Sabres were replaced by the Northrop F-5F combat trainer.

South Africa

During the latter months of the Korean War, the pilots of No 2 Squadron, South African Air Force, had gained considerable combat experience with the F-86F Sabre during operations with the USAF 18th Tactical Fighter Wing, so that the SAAF already had a large nucleus of trained F-86 pilots when the decision was taken in 1956

to replace the Service's de Havilland Vampires (Mks 5 and 9) with the Canadair Sabre Mk 6. Thirty-four aircraft were delivered, equipping No 1 Squadron at Pietersberg and No 2 Squadron at Waterkloof. In June 1963, No 2 'Cheetah' Squadron began to re-equip with the Dassault Mirage IIICZ, its Sabres being assigned to No 1 Squadron. Because of a wide-ranging arms embargo endorsed by the United Nations, the SAAF's re-equipment programme was subjected to numerous delays, and No 1 Squadron retained its Sabres until 1977, when it re-equipped with the Mirage F.1AZ. Twelve of its Sabre 6s were transferred to No 85

Spain was one of the biggest F-86F users outside the United States. This example belonged to the 6th Day Fighter Wing.

F-86F of the 111th Fighter Squadron, Spanish Air Force.

Spain

Advanced Flying School, also at Pietersberg, but these had been replaced by Mirage IIIs by the end of 1979.

Although Spain did not become a member of NATO until the early 1980s, the Spanish Government under General Franco was firmly pro-Western and, in return for the use by the United States of three key air bases and a naval base, received substantial quantities of American aid. In fact, Spain was one of the principal users of the Sabre outside NATO, three Wings totalling nine squadrons being equipped with the F-86F.

The first batch of an eventual 225 aircraft, all ex-USAF, was delivered to CASA's Madrid factory for overhaul in September 1955, and the first thirteen refurbished F-86Fs were handed over to the *Ejercito del Aire* (Air Force) at Getafe on 6 October 1956. Deliveries proceeded at a rapid rate, and 152 Sabres were in service by the end of January 1957. The Sabres equipped Nos 11, 12 and 14 Day Interceptor Wings and remained first-line equipment until 1970, when, beginning with *Escuadron 101 de Caza* at Valencia-Manises, they were replaced by Mirages.

Thailand

The last of forty F-86F Sabres was delivered to the Royal Thai Air Force (RTAF) in March 1962, replacing the F-84G Thunderjets of No 12 Squadron of the 1st Wing at Don Muang and also equipping No 13 Squadron at the same base. Some F-86L Sabres were also assigned to No 12 Squadron in 1964, providing the RTAF with a limited all-weather interception capability. In April 1966 No 13 Squadron began re-equipping with the Northrop F-5A, its F-86Fs going to No 43 Squadron of the 4th Wing at Takli. Sabres continued in RTAF service until the mid-1970s, when No 12 Squadron converted to the counter-insurgency role with the OV-10 Bronco and the 43rd Squadron was deactivated. As part of the SEATO forces, the RTAF F-86s exercised regularly with the RAAF Sabre Wing at Butterworth and also, from time to time, with RAF Hunter FGA.9s from No 20 Squadron, Singapore.

Tunisia

Twelve F-86F Sabres were supplied by the USA to the Tunisian Republican Air Force in 1969, but by 1975 attrition had substantially reduced this small force and the survivors were used mainly in the training role until 1984, when they were replaced by Northrop F-5Es.

Venezuela

One of the better-equipped of the Latin American air arms, the Venezuelan Air Force operated two day fighter squadrons of F-86F Sabres, delivered in 1959–60. In 1966, the Venezuelan government purchased forty-seven ex-*Luftwaffe* F-86K Sabres, which replaced the de Havilland Vampire FB.5 in *Escuadrones de Caza-Bombardeo* 35 and 36. The latter unit's F-86Ks were replaced in the mid-1970s by Mirage IIIEV and 5V aircraft, but *Escuadron* 35's Sabres were not withdrawn until 1981, when they were replaced by CF-5As.

Yugoslavia

After refurbishment in the United Kingdom, seventy-nine ex-RAF Canadair Sabre Mk 4s were allocated to the Yugoslav Air Force in 1956–7. One of these (ex-XB775) was written-off at Naples during the delivery flight on 19 January 1957. Some 130 F-86D/K Sabres were also obtained from NATO stocks in the late 1960s. The Sabre Mk 4 was replaced in Yugoslav service by the MiG-21, but the all-weather Sabres, the survivors, concentrated in two squadrons at Skopje, were not withdrawn from first-line duties until 1982, by which time the combat element of the Yugoslav Air Force was equipped almost entirely with MiG-21s.

Chapter 12
Pakistan's Sabres at War

AT THE beginning of 1954, the Royal Pakistan Air Force (RPAF) had been in existence for less than seven years. There could, however, be no doubt about its skill and professionalism. It was organized and trained by Royal Air Force personnel on secondment, and its first three commanders-in-chief were senior RAF officers: Air Vice-Marshal A.L.A. Perry-Keene, AV-M R.L.R. Atcherley, and AV-M L.W. Cannon. While the first two laid the foundations of this small, highly-trained air arm, it was AV-M Cannon who reorganized and revitalized the structure of the RPAF, instituting long-term policies to cover future expansion, recruitment and training.

What the RPAF lacked was modern equipment. Its sole jet fighter squadron was equipped with the Vickers Supermarine Attacker, thirty-six of which were delivered in 1951, and three squadrons operated piston-engined Hawker Fury fighter-bombers. Although the Attacker performed reasonably well in RPAF service it suffered from a number of technical problems, the most serious of which involved the undercarriage, and several aircraft were lost in landing accidents.

It was the Korean War, and growing communist influence and aggression in other Far Eastern theatres, that gave impetus to the military re-equipment programme in Pakistan. To provide collective security in South-East Asia the South-East Asia Treaty Organization (SEATO) was formed in 1954, the member nations being Australia, France, New Zealand, Pakistan, the Philippines, Thailand, the United Kingdom and the United States. It was also envisaged that Pakistan would be a signatory to the

Central Treaty Organization (CENTO), based on the former Baghdad Pact, when this came into being later in the 1950s, although CENTO was an economic organization rather than a military one.

On 19 May 1954, as a preliminary to its participation in SEATO, Pakistan signed a Mutual Defence Assistance Pact with the United States. The result was an almost immediate influx of American military equipment and the secondment of a US Military Advisory Group, which began to switch over the RPAF to American methods of training and organization. A quantity of North American T-6G Texan trainers was supplied to the RPAF College at Risalpur, and the first of fifteen Lockheed T-33A jet trainers was delivered to No 2 (Fighter Conversion) Squadron at Mauripur where they replaced Hawker Furies and some earlier Tempest IIs, inherited from India at the time of partition in 1947.

As far as combat aircraft were concerned, it was proposed to establish an operational element, by the end of 1957, of four day fighter Wings, each with two squadrons of twelve F-86F Sabres, plus one Sabre for the Wing leader and one T-33A per Wing. Alfa Wing (Nos 18 and 19 Squadrons) was to be based at Mauripur; Bravo Wing (Nos 11 and 15 Squadrons) at Peshawar; Cocoa Wing (Nos 16 and 17 Squadrons) at Sarghoda; and Delta Wing (Nos 5 and 14 Squadrons) at Samungli.

During the transition period, the RPAF was still commanded by a RAF officer, AV-M A.W.B. McDonald, who succeeded AV-M Cannon in June 1955. Deliveries of F-86Fs to operational units began later that year, the first squadrons to re-equip being Nos 5 and 14 Squadrons. By the end of 1956

No 11 Squadron had exchanged its Attackers for Sabres, and four more squadrons, Nos 15, 16, 17 and 18, had been formed as planned. No 19 Squadron formed at a later date. The initial nucleus of RPAF Sabre pilots trained in the United States; thereafter, all jet conversion was undertaken by No 2 (Fighter Conversion) Squadron at Mauripur, where, after 200–220 hours on the T-6G at Risalpur, pilots flew eighty hours on the T-33A during the first three months of the course and fifty hours on the Sabre during the last three months.

On 26 March 1956, Pakistan was proclaimed an Islamic Republic and the Air Force dropped its 'Royal' prefix. By 23 July 1957, when the first Pakistani C-in-C, Air Marshal M. Asghar Khan, assumed command, the fighter strength of the PAF had doubled. Only one unit retained piston-engined equipment; this was No 9 Squadron, which continued to operate Hawker Furies for police duties on the North-West Frontier until it converted to Lockheed F-104A Starfighters in 1960.

In the early 1960s, notwithstanding the fact that relations with India were fast deteriorating, Pakistan's main area of concern was the North-West Frontier with Afghanistan, which had been receiving military equipment – including modern jet aircraft – from the Soviet Union. Early in 1965 the Royal Afghan Air Force possessed six squadrons of MiG-17s, with another squadron working up on MiG-21s, and the PAF's Sabres flew regular border patrols ready to counter any potential air threat. But when a show of force finally came, it was between Pakistan and India.

In February 1965, Indian forces occupied the northern part of the Rann of Kutch, a desolate area of disputed salt flats on the Indo-Pakistan border south of Kashmir. During the weeks that followed there were several skirmishes between rival armoured forces, which ended late in April after a flurry of diplomatic activity. Air power – apart from light observation aircraft and helicopters – played no part in these actions, both sides at this stage being eager to avoid escalation, but the Sabre force was brought to alert status and the aircraft ordered to their wartime dispersals, together with the PAF's small force of Martin B-57 jet bombers.

There were several cross-border incursions, however, by Indian aircraft, and on 24 April a section of Sabres was scrambled to intercept a radar contact fifty miles inside Pakistani territory and apparently heading for Karachi. The contact turned out to be an IAF Dassault Ouragan, whose pilot lowered his flaps and undercarriage when the Sabres made a warning pass and came down near the village of Jangshahi, wiping off his landing gear in the process. It transpired that the Ouragan pilot, Flt Lt Rana Sikka of No 51 Auxiliary Squadron, had got lost in poor visibility and strayed across the border by mistake.

In July 1965, command of the PAF was assumed by Air Marshal M. Nur Khan. His appointment came at a time when the Pakistan Government was actively pursuing a plan to infiltrate the disputed province of Kashmir with some 8,000 guerrilla and regular forces, and he at once realized that, once this action had been taken, nothing short of full PAF commitment would become necessary. An Intelligence assessment of the IAF's war plan indicated that the Indians would seek first of all to neutralize the PAF, then undertake a sustained interdiction campaign against Pakistani communications and war industry, with petrol, oil and lubricant (POL) facilities high on the list of target priorities.

The biggest problem confronting the PAF, which was heavily outnumbered, was to deploy its forces so that the requirements of air defence and battlefield air superiority could be adequately met. It was finally decided to concentrate almost the whole of the Sabre force in the Sargodha–Peshawar area, assigning only one squadron to the defence of Karachi; this would result in the maximum economy of force and also place the Sabres within comfortable reach of the battle area. Combat air patrols (CAPs) were to be flown by elements of three aircraft, one F-104 Starfighter and two F-86Fs, all armed with Sidewinder AAMs; the F-104 would provide top cover. As the PAF had 100 Sabres and only ten Starfighters the number of CAPs would be limited, but the arrangement was judged to be adequate. In any case, only twenty-two Sabres were as yet equipped to carry the Sidewinder.

The majority of the Sabre force was assigned to attacks on Indian forward airfields, the first scheduled to take place just before sunset on the first day of hostilities. The object was to inflict the maximum amount of damage, at the same time ensuring that nightfall would limit the Indian response. Further airfield attacks were to take place at sunrise, pressure being maintained by the PAF's B-57 force during the night. Because of the range involved – Sargodha was more than 120 miles from the Indian frontier – and the need to carry external fuel tanks to permit sufficient time over target, no rockets would be carried; attacks would be made using guns only. Twelve Sabres would be assigned to each target, the whole force crossing the Indian border simultaneously.

On 31 August 1965, the eve of the Pakistani offensive into Kashmir (Operation *Grand Slam*), the serviceability state of the PAF's Sabre force was high, only eight of the 100 aircraft being out of the line for repair and overhaul. Of the ninety-two serviceable aircraft, thirty – including the Sidewinder-equipped Sabres – were with Nos 5, 11 and 15 Squadrons at Sargodha in the Punjab, alongside the F-104s of No 9 Squadron; No 19 was at Peshawar with fourteen aircraft; and Nos 16, 17 and 18 were at Mauripur with thirty-six aircraft, although Nos 17 and 18 Squadrons would quickly redeploy to Sargodha in support of the airfield attack effort; and No 14 Squadron was at Tezgaon, near Dacca in East Pakistan, with twelve aircraft.

It was anticipated that once the fighting

in Kashmir began, there would be an immediate challenge to any Pakistani bid for air superiority from the Indian Air Force's (IAF) Hawker Hunter F. Mk 56 fighters, whose performance was superior to that of the F-86F in most respects. The IAF had 118 Hunters, divided between four squadrons, and two of these – Nos 7 and 27 Squadrons – were based close to the disputed Kashmir border at Halwara, south of Amritsar. When hostilities opened on 1 September, however, the first Indian aircraft to be committed to attacks on advancing Pakistani armour were Canberra B(I) 58 bombers, de Havilland Vampires and Dassault Ouragans.

The first contact between the opposing air forces came in the late afternoon of 1 September, when a section of two Sabres flown by Sqn Ldr Sarfaraz Rafiqui, OC No 5 Squadron, and Flt Lt Imtiaz Bhatti, No 15 Squadron, intercepted a small force of Vampires and Canberras over the battle area. Two Vampires were quickly destroyed by Sqn Ldr Rafiqui, and the other two by his wingman. There were no further air actions on that day; nor were there any on 2 September, when no sightings of Indian aircraft were reported.

The PAF's airfield attack plan was now postponed, and from first light on 2 September part of the Sabre force was employed in attacking Indian strongpoints in the Jaurian area with 2.75 in rockets, twenty-eight of which were carried by each aircraft. Attacks were also made on Indian columns, the PAF pilots claiming the destruction of four tanks and about twenty soft-skinned vehicles. During the course of the day, ten Sabres of No 17 Squadron were redeployed from Mauripur to Sargodha to strengthen the ground-attack force.

On the morning of 3 September, PAF Sabres had their first encounter with a modern IAF combat type, the Hawker Siddeley Gnat lightweight fighter. Two Sabres and an F-104, all armed with Sidewinders, were on CAP from Sargodha when four Gnats climbed past the Sabres. The latter, led by Flt Lt Yusaf Khan, turned after the Indian aircraft, but Khan's wing-man, Fg Off Butt, was forced to break off when one of his drop tanks refused to jettison. Khan obtained missile tone on a Gnat, but then his Sabre was hit by three 30 mm cannon shells from another Gnat which had got on his tail. Butt's obstinate fuel tank at last fell away and he returned to rejoin his leader, the two Sabres engaging the Gnats – which now numbered six – in a turning fight down to less than 1,500 feet. Then the CAP F-104 arrived from high altitude, and although it could not match the Sabres and Gnats in a turning battle its pilot made several high-speed passes at the Indian fighters, causing them to break away and head for friendly territory. One of the Gnats was intercepted by a second Starfighter and landed on a disused PAF airfield at Pasrur, where it was later captured intact; its pilot claimed to have experienced technical trouble. Meanwhile, Flt Lt Khan nursed his damaged F-86F back to Sargodha, were he made a tricky landing without the use of brakes.

On 4 September the emphasis was once again on ground support operations, three flights of four Sabres – two armed with rockets and the third with napalm – attacking Indian artillery positions and convoys. It was during these operations that the Sabre force suffered its first loss when the aircraft flown by Fg Off N.M. Butt, who had taken part in the action against the Gnats the day before, was hit shortly after making an attack on an Indian HQ near Jammu. Butt ejected and landed safely near friendly troops. Butt at first believed that he had been shot down by AA fire, but it later transpired that an Indian aircraft, possibly a Gnat, had been responsible. The PAF also mounted thirty-four CAP sorties on 4 September, but although Pakistani radar stations tracked numerous Indian aircraft – including some identified as MiG-21s by their speed – there were no engagements.

In the early hours of 6 September, following a day of relative quiet that saw only sixteen sorties by PAF Sabres, the Indian Army launched a major offensive towards Lahore, supported by diversionary attacks, and the war began in earnest. The offensive was supported by substantial numbers of Indian aircraft, but their attacks were unco-ordinated and there was little evidence of a coherent air/ground plan of action. For the first time, PAF pilots began to encounter Dassault Mystère IVA fighter-bombers, the Vampires having been withdrawn from operations following their mauling of 1 September. One Mystère was shot down by a Sidewinder launched by a CAP F-104 early on the 6th.

Later in the morning, Sabres carried out rocket attacks on Indian armoured columns advancing towards Lahore. From noon on 6 September, a state of open war existed between India and Pakistan, and it was now decided to implement the planned series of air strikes on Indian Air Force bases. The decision was not taken without some misgivings, because the attacks were certain to attract large-scale IAF retaliation. One major concern was aircraft availability; the threat of IAF strikes meant that a high proportion of the Sabre force would have to be assigned to air defence, and there were fears that the number available for the strikes against Indian airfields and their associated radar facilities would not be adequate. To alleviate the situation, twelve Sabres of No 18 Squadron flew to Sargodha from Mauripur, but they arrived late in the afternoon and four of them had to be taken out of the line so that various defects could be rectified. Apart from this, some of the Sargodha F-86Fs had been carrying out further ground-attack missions during the afternoon and were still returning to base; it would take time to refuel and re-arm them.

The only force fully prepared to go on schedule was at Peshawar, where eight Sabres of No 19 Squadron – which so far had been committed only to air defence tasks – were standing by to take-off for their assigned target, the IAF airfield at Pathankot. When it was decided that the attack was to go ahead as planned, the Peshawar force got airborne on schedule at 16.15 hours; the problem was that the Sargodha Sabres were nowhere near ready, so that the original plan involving a simultaneous border crossing by the whole Sabre force in order to achieve maximum surprise was severely disrupted.

The eight pilots of No 19 Squadron, led by Sqn Ldr S.S. Haider, were briefed to cross into Indian territory at 32,000 feet and then descend to low level twenty miles from the target. Two Sidewinder-armed Sabres were to provide top cover at 15,000 feet. The airfield attack would be made using guns only, each aircraft carrying 1,800 rounds of armour-piercing and incendiary ammunition, and each pilot was to make two passes.

The Sabre pilots arrived at Pathankot to find a number of aircraft dispersed in blast pens around the airfield perimeter; these were attacked and various installations strafed, including the control tower. After the attack the pilots claimed the destruction of nine MiG-21s, five Mystère IVAs and a Fairchild C-119 transport; in fact no MiGs were present, but the C-119 and several Mystères were definitely destroyed. All the Sabres recovered safely to the nearest PAF airfield, which was Sarghoda. No opposition was encountered apart from some light AA.

Meanwhile, the strike from Sargodha had been dogged by misfortune. Only eight Sabres could be mustered to attack the two IAF airfields at Adampur and Halwara, and shortly before take-off this number was further reduced to six when two of the aircraft became unserviceable. Con-

The Hunter F.Mk 56 was the F-86F's main opponent during the 1965 conflict. The British fighter was superior on most counts, but less manoeuvrable than the lighter Sabre.

sequently, only three Sabres of No 11 Squadron set out for Adampur, headed by the CO, Sqn Ldr M.M. Alam, while the three aircraft of No 5 Squadron led by Sqn Ldr S.A. Rafiqui, made for Halwara.

Flying at low level across the Punjab, the small Adampur force met with trouble a few seconds short of its Initial Point at Taran Taran, south of Amritsar, when the Sabres were engaged by four Hunters. A low-level, low-speed turning fight developed; Alam fired at the No 4 Hunter, which flicked into the ground and exploded, although this may have been the result of the Indian pilot losing control. The combat tightened up even further as the opposing pilots lowered their flaps in frantic endeavours to get on one anothers' tails; at this speed and height the Sabre was marginally more manoeuvrable than the Hunter and Alam succeeded in shooting down a second aircraft. Two more Hunters were claimed as damaged by the other two Sabre pilots, Sqn Ldr A.U. Ahmed and Flt Lt S.A.A. Hatmi.

With no prospect now of attacking Adampur in the gathering dusk, and the danger that more Indian fighters might shortly arrive, Alam called off the mission and the pilots made their exits from the combat area at low level. On the way home the Sabre flight encountered another pair of Hunters and fired at one of them with inconclusive results.

A Pakistan Air Force F-86F explodes under the gunfire of an Indian Air Force Hunter during the war of 1965.

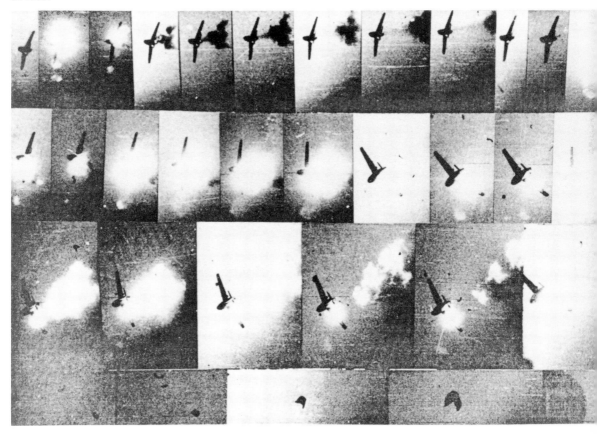

A couple of minutes later, Alam's flight made visual contact with the three Sabres of No 5 Squadron, which had just crossed the border en route for Halwara, and they were called up over the R/T with a warning that Indian fighters were up in strength. As it turned out, Sqn Ldr Rafiqui's aircraft reached the target area without meeting any opposition; their problem was that they were unable to locate Halwara in the gathering darkness.

As they circled at low level, vainly trying to find the objective, Rafiqui sighted two Hunters at twelve o'clock high and decided to attack them. Covered by his Nos 2 and 3, Flt Lt Cecil Choudhry and Flt Lt Yunus Hussain, Rafiqui closed on the lead Hunter and shot it down. As the other aircraft broke sharply away six more Hunters appeared, closing rapidly from port and starboard; Rafiqui turned in behind the first pair and fired a short burst at one of them, then his guns jammed. Choudhry, meanwhile, engaged a second pair of Hunters, hitting one in the port wing; it pulled up steeply and the pilot ejected. The other used its superior acceleration to disengage.

Choudhry, who was down to less than 200 feet, was then attacked by two more Hunters, both of which passed underneath him. The Indian No 2 misjudged his height and hit the ground with his wingtip, his aircraft exploding. By virtue of some magnificent low-speed flying Choudhry caused another attacking Hunter to overshoot and fired at it; the Hunter exploded. Looking round, he saw a Sabre and a Hunter sparring with one another in a scissors manoeuvre; a moment later the Hunter burst into flames and went down.

The successful pilot was Yunus Hussain. There was no sign of Rafiqui, so Choudhry and Hussain set out for home. As they did so they were attacked by two more Hunters from six o'clock high, and one of them shot Hussain down in flames. Choudhry, harrassed by the two Hunters and two more which came up to join the unequal fight, stayed at low level and gradually worked his way towards the border; the Hunters lost him in the shadows. On reaching Lahore he climbed to 20,000 feet and headed for Sargodha, expecting his fuel to run out several miles short of base. In fact, he was on his final approach to land when the engine flamed out, and he was able to make a successful dead-stick landing, the sole survivor of the No 5 Squadron effort.

The anticipated IAF response came just before midnight. During the next four and a half hours at least fourteen Canberras penetrated Pakistan air space, heading for the airfields at Rawalpindi and Sargodha. The Canberras, which were operating out of Agra, attacked in stream from 30,000 feet, dropping either six 1,000 lb HE bombs or a single 4,000 lb bomb. Bombs fell near both targets but caused no damage to military installations; in fact, many failed to explode. Three F-104s made abortive attempts to intercept the bombers; two F-86s were also scrambled from Mauripur and one of these crashed shortly after take-off, killing its pilot.

The first IAF daylight attack on Sargodha, mounted by six Mystère IVAs soon after sunrise, took the defences by surprise but failed completely to exploit this advantage. The Mystères made a single ragged pass over the airfield, firing their underwing rockets and cannon indiscriminately, and failed to hit any of the 80-odd aircraft on the base, including four Sabres and two F-104s on the Operational Readiness Platform at the end of the run-way. One Mystère was shot down by light AA and another by a CAP Starfighter several miles south-east of the airfield. The Starfighter was itself engaged by a second Mystère, whose pilot, showing consider-able skill and courage, pressed home his attack and hit the F-104 with cannon fire, damaging its controls. The PAF pilot ejected safely.

Soon afterwards, six Hunters were reported to be approaching Sargodha at low level. Four F-86s and one F-104 were already airborne, having been scrambled on CAP after the first attack; with the Starfighter providing top cover, the Sabres intercepted the Hunters as they were running in towards Sargodha. The Sabre leader, Sqn Ldr M.M. Alam, and his No 2, Fg Off M. Akhtar, pursued the Hunters across the airfield and closed on the rearmost pair as they turned eastward. Alam fired two Sidewinders at them; one of the missiles fell away harmlessly, but the other appeared to have damaged the second low-flying Hunter, whose pilot pulled up and ejected.

With the other Sabre pair orbiting some distance away to the south-west, Alam and his wingman continued their pursuit of the remaining Hunters, catching up with them just beyond the Chenab river. Seeing the threat, the Indian pilots broke left in line astern, putting the Sabres in an excellent position to turn in behind them. What followed was one of the most remarkable achievements in the history of air combat. In less than 30 seconds, firing in short bursts while pulling up to 5g in the turn, Sqn Ldr Alam destroyed four Hunters. At close range, the combination of the Sabre's A-4 radar ranging gunsight and battery of six 0.50 in. machine-guns proved very effective. One burst punctured a Hunter's fuel tanks and the second ignited the escaping kerosene, and that was that. Only one Hunter escaped. As on the previous day, Alam – a highly experienced pilot with about 1,400 hours on type – had exploited the Sabre's low-speed turning qualities to the full. The Hunter pilots, instead of breaking in opposite directions and drawing the Sabres to higher altitude, had tried to match their attacker's manoeuvrability, and had paid for their mistake with their lives.

The third attack on Sargodha came at 09.45, when four Mystères evaded the F-86/F-104 CAP and attacked the airfield with rockets and cannon fire. One Sabre was destroyed and some installations damaged; the Indian aircraft escaped unharmed. The final daylight attack of 7 September, again by four Mystères, was made late in the afternoon. No damage was caused to the airfield, and on this occasion one Mystère was shot down by ground fire and another by a CAP Sabre flown by Flt Lt A.H. Malik, who destroyed it with a Sidewinder.

Meanwhile, 1,000 miles away in East Pakistan, the twelve Sabres of No 14 Squadron at Tezgaon had begun their own war. As part of the PAF's airfield attack plan, the squadron was briefed to hit the IAF base at Kalaikunda, about 220 miles away and 60 miles to the west of Calcutta. On the night of 6/7 September, Canberras from this airfield penetrated as far as Dacca and dropped a number of bombs, causing light damage and a few casualties, and at first light a Sabre CAP was ordered up to search for Indian Canberras and Hunters which were reported to be attacking Chittagong airfield and the new international airport at Kurmitola, north of Dacca. While orbiting over the capital under very low cloud, the pilot of one of the Sabres, Flt Lt Aziz, lost control and dived into the ground, losing his life.

The attack on Kalaikunda was carried out by five Sabres, whose pilots found fourteen Canberras drawn up on the tarmac and three Hunters parked on the ORP. During the strike the pilots claimed the destruction of ten Canberras, with two more and two Hunters damaged, and although this claim may have been exaggerated the attack undoubtedly caused much damage. A second strike, by four Sabres, was mounted four hours later and was intercepted by nine Hunters, one of which shot down the F-86 flown by Fg Off Afzal Khan. The other three Sabres returned to base safely.

In the west, while the Sargodha F-86 squadrons had been preoccupied with air defence throughout the day, No 19 Squadron at Peshawar had been tasked with armed reconnaissance and close support. In the late afternoon, four Sabres led by Sqn Ldr Haider strafed Srinagar airfield through intense AA fire, destroying two C-47 Dakotas and a DHC Caribou. A second attack, again led by Haider, was made against Pathankot airfield by five Sabres, but no worthwhile targets could be discerned in the gathering dusk and the mission proved abortive.

Following its losses in daylight attacks on 7 September, the IAF's offensive against PAF airfields was carried out entirely by night-flying Canberras. These operations were helped by the fact that the PAF had no night-fighters as such; the best it could do was to put up its F-104s and those aircraft of the Sabre force which were modified to carry Sidewinder AAMs and hope that ground radar could put them somewhere in the vicinity of a target. The PAF pilots' task was not made easier by the Canberra's Orange Putter tail warning radar, which alerted the crew when an F-104's AI radar was locked on and enabled them to take early evasive action.

Having no AI radar, the PAF Sabre pilots who tried to intercept the elusive Canberras relied entirely on GCI and the infra-red homing unit of the Sidewinder AAM. If the pilot heard the missile tone, indicating that the seeker head was activated, it meant that GCI had placed him a couple of miles or less astern of his target; all he could do then was launch his missiles blind.

At best it was an unsatisfactory method, but on the night of 14/15 September Flt Lt Cecil Choudhry used it successfully to intercept a Canberra over Lahore. The Indian aircraft was flying at 31,000 feet, cruising at 0.7M, and GCI placed Choudhry behind it. He acquired the first missile tone as he pulled up through 30,000 feet, searching vainly for the Canberra's contrails in the moonlight, and launched a Sidewinder. After a long wait he saw the missile self-destruct, and knew that he had missed. His second AAM, however, found its target, and although he did not see the Canberra go down it was later confirmed to have crashed by All-India Radio. One other Canberra was shot down at night, on 21/22 September, by an F-104.

From 8 September, Pakistan's counter-air effort against Indian airfields was taken over by the PAF's American-built version of the British Canberra jet bomber, the Martin B-57, which left the Sabre force free to mount an increasing number of ground support missions and fighter sweeps over the battle area. On average, requests for close support from Pakistan Army units were met within 90 minutes, although the PAF pilots suffered from poor air/ground liaison and a lack of forward air controllers. Target marking procedures were virtually non-existent, which meant that pilots had to spend lengthy periods flying around the battle area at low level, where they were vulnerable to light AA, while they sought their objectives. Despite this, not one F-86 was lost to enemy AA during 500 ground-attack sorties, although fifty-eight returned to base with varying degrees of battle damage.

Indian Air Force Gnats were encountered on several occasions during the following days, the IAF having apparently assigned these diminutive aircraft to CAP while the Hunters concentrated on ground attack. On 10 September, four Sabres from Sargodha, led by Sqn Ldr Muniruddin Ahmed, were on CAP over the Kasur area, about ten miles inside Indian territory, when their controlling radar station at Sakesar warned them of enemy aircraft in the vicinity. These turned out to be two Gnats, which were already in a pursuit curve by the time the PAF pilots spotted them. The Gnats overshot the second pair of Sabres and opened fire on Sqn Ldr Ahmed and his No 2, Flt Lt Bhatti. Ahmed broke and got on the tail of the leading Gnat, which began to smoke under his gunfire and went into a spin. The second Gnat, instead of breaking off what was now a very unequal combat, turned back into the fight and opened fire on Ahmed. The Gnat was engaged by Flt Lt Choudhry, who was flying No 3, and the Indian fighter accelerated away. Choudhry launched a Sidewinder at it, but with no result.

From 10 September, the ground attack effort by the Sabre squadrons at Sargodha was placed on a more professional footing with the establishment of a dedicated Strike Wing; this was No 32 Wing, comprising Nos 17 and 18 Squadrons with a total of eighteen aircraft. The Strike Wing was given its own airfield dispersal area, where the Sabres could be turned round quickly between sorties. Anti-armour operations featured high on the Strike Wing's list of target priorities, and for this purpose the Sabres were armed with four jettisonable underwing pods, each containing seven 2.75 inch Folding-Fin Aircraft Rockets (FFAR) with High Explosive Anti-Tank (HEAT) warheads, or with eight .5 inch rockets as an alternative load.

The first ground attack operations by the Strike Wing as an entity involved a series of strikes on 10 and 11 September on Indian armoured columns in the Samba area, just inside the Kashmir border. During the two-day period No 32 Wing claimed nineteen tanks and more than 100 other vehicles destroyed; this may have been an over-estimate, but the fact remained that the planned Indian armoured thrust in this area did not materialize.

The PAF ground-attack effort – which was shared to a limited extent by armed T-33 jet trainers and by B-57s – continued unabated during the following week, and on 13 September train-busting was added to No 32 Wing's activities. Four Sabres led by Sqn Ldr A.U. Ahmed, carrying out their second mission of the day – the first had been a strike on Indian armour and artillery in the Chawinda–Narowal sector at first light – attacked rolling stock in the goods yard of Gurdaspur station and hit an ammunition train, which exploded with spectacular results. Sqn Ldr Ahmed's aircraft was damaged in the blast and he was forced to eject over the front line. When Pakistani forces reached him he was dead – shot, so it was thought, as he came down under his parachute. Friendly fire may have been responsible.

On 13 September two IAF Gnats again put in an appearance, climbing from Halwara to intercept four F-86Fs on CAP at 20,000 feet over Amritsar. In the ensuing turning fight, which brought the aircraft down to 3,000 feet, one Gnat was shot down in flames by Flt Lt Yusuf Ali Khan and a second damaged by Flt Lt Bhatti. The Gnat regained its base, but according to All-India Radio its pilot later died of wounds sustained during the combat. Four Gnats were also encountered by CAP Sabres on 14 September, but on this occasion the Indian fighters refused combat.

On 15 September, the Sargodha Strike Wing launched an intensive series of attacks against enemy armour in the Chawinda sector. Ground fire was intense and almost all the Sabres were damaged, several of them severely, but Herculean efforts by PAF maintenance personnel had the majority airworthy by the next day, when they were in action against Indian armoured columns on the Samba–Bajpur road. In two days of air strikes, the F-86F pilots claimed the destruction of twenty-eight tanks and about 160 soft-skinned vehicles; the Strike Wing was now mounting up to forty sorties a day.

While the Strike Wing maintained pressure against Indian ground forces, the other Sargodha units succeeded for the most part in keeping the Indian Air Force at arm's length with regular combat air patrols. On 16 September, two Sabres led by Sqn Ldr Alam were flying CAP at 20,000 feet close to the enemy airfields of Halwara and Adampur when two Hunters came up to challenge them. The Hunters used their superior climb to get above the Sabres and then came down in a fast dive at about 0.98M, zooming up in a yo-yo manoeuvre as the Sabres broke into a turn. Rolling into another dive, the Hunters went down to about 14,000 feet with the Sabres behind them. One continued straight down but the other pulled up to 20,000 feet with Alam in pursuit. Turning behind the Hunter, Alam fired several short bursts and his opponent burst into flames. Turning away, Alam saw the second Hunter in pursuit of his wing-man, Fg Off M.I. Shaukat, and went after it. The Indian pilot, seeing the threat developing from astern, dived away rapidly towards Halwara. Alam launched two Sidewinders, one of which scored a hit on the Hunter's wing root. It was Alam's ninth and last victory of the war, a success marred by the fact that his wingman had been shot down. Shaukat, in fact, ejected and became a prisoner of war.

On 18 September there was another encounter between Sabres and Gnats, four of which were scrambled to intercept a similar number of F-86Fs on CAP in the Taran Taran sector. The engagement began at 25,000 feet, the opposing aircraft turning in pairs in a large circle, and continued down to 2,000 feet with neither side gaining an advantage until one of the PAF pilots, Flt Lt S.A.A. Hatmi, got on the tail of a Gnat and launched a Sidewinder. The Gnat began to burn and dived into the ground. Then a second Gnat crashed, the victim of Indian AA fire, and the remaining pair flew away.

On the following day, more Gnats evaded the CAP screen and attacked Sabres of the Sargodha Strike Wing which were in action against Indian armour in the Sialkot area. One Sabre was badly damaged by 30 mm cannon shells but recovered to Sargodha, and a Gnat was shot down. Its pilot ejected and was captured.

The last fighter combat of the three-week war occurred on 20 September, when the IAF came up in strength to oppose four CAP Sabres at 20,000 feet between Kasur and Lahore. First to appear were four Hunters, one of which dived away after being hit and damaged by Sqn Ldr S.A. Changezi; he saw it hit the ground. Then four Gnats arrived and one of them engaged the Sabre flown by Flt Lt A.H. Malik, hitting it with 30 mm fire. Shells from two more Gnats struck the Sabre in quick succession and Malik just managed to keep it under control until he reached friendly territory, where he ejected. The remaining three Hunters and the four Gnats continued to do battle with the other three Sabres. One PAF pilot, Flt Lt S.N.A. Jilani, managed to turn inside a Hunter and

fired a long burst into it at close range: the Indian fighter went down in flames. The remaining IAF aircraft disappeared into the dusk.

Although no further engagements were reported during the last two days of the Indo-Pakistan conflict, Indian aircraft continued to appear over Kashmir and the PAF's Sabres and F-104s went on mounting CAP. In the case of No 32 Wing, the final effort involved a series of attacks on Indian heavy artillery that was shelling Lahore. A ceasefire came into effect in the early hours of 23 September.

In East Pakistan, following further IAF bombing raids, No 14 Squadron's Sabres had carried out a series of airfield attacks, the first on 10 September against Baghdogra, where they destroyed a C-119 transport, a Hunter, a helicopter and a Vampire T.55 trainer. On 14 September, four-Sabre flights also attacked Barrackpore, near Calcutta, and Argatala, as well as a radar station at Rampurhat. During the whole series of airfield strikes, No 14 Squadron claimed to have destroyed twenty-four Indian aircraft on the ground for the loss of two Sabres.

The PAF lost thirteen F-86Fs during the war, and of these only seven were claimed in air combat. Nevertheless, it left the remainder of the Sabre force in poor shape, and the problem was compounded by the fact that all US military aid had been severed on the outbreak of hostilities. This meant that the PAF had to rely on existing stocks of spare parts, and these had never been maintained at a particularly high level. Worst affected were the Sabres of Nos 17 and 18 Squadrons, whose aircraft had been subjected to severe stress and battle damage during their ground-attack operations.

In October 1965, the Chinese People's Republic offered to supply modern combat aircraft to Pakistan, the principal type involved being the Shenyang F-6 (MiG-19). The offer was accepted, and by early 1966 the pilots of No 11 Squadron were converting to the new type; two new squadrons, Nos 23 and 25, were also formed to operate it. The F-6 seemed well suited to Pakistan's air defence requirements; it had powerful engines, a good thrust-to-weight ratio, a good rate of climb, and provided the answer to the problem of intercepting high-speed intruders from airfields just across Pakistan's borders. Lacking geographical depth, Pakistan was particularly vulnerable to hit-and-run tactics.

The Sabre, however, remained the PAF's primary ground-attack aircraft, and Pakistan went to considerable lengths to obtain replacements for its more weary F-86Fs. In 1966, ninety surplus *Luftwaffe* Canadair Sabre Mk 6s were bought by an arms purchasing firm in Switzerland and then ostensibly sold to Iran. The Iranian government, pleading a lack of technical facilities (which was true, since the combat arm of the Iranian Air Force at that time consisted of only three squadrons of F-84G Thunderjets) sent the Sabres to Pakistan 'for overhaul'. They never returned; instead, they were used to re-equip Nos 17, 18 and 19 Squadrons, whose discarded aircraft were cannibalized to provide spares for the rest of the F-86F fleet.

This left Nos 5, 14, 15 and 16 Squadrons still operating the F-86F, mainly in the close support role, but in 1968 No 5 Squadron began re-equipping with Pakistan's latest combat aircraft acquisition, the Dassault Mirage IIIEP.

In 1971 East Pakistan, whose social and economic links with the western part of the country had been growing steadily weaker, declared independence as the new state of Bangladesh. West Pakistan tried to counter this with savage repression, but her under-strength army in the east, already under pressure from Bangladeshi irregulars, found itself in an untenable position when faced with Indian military intervention. In December 1971 India and Pakistan once again found themselves at war, the Pakistan Army attacking India's defences in Kashmir and the Punjab in a bid to divert some of her strength from the eastern front, where the Indian Army was making skilful use of airborne forces to achieve its objectives.

When hostilities broke out on 3 December there were eighty-eight Sabres, mostly Mk 6s, on the PAF Order of Battle with first-line units, and these featured prominently in a series of pre-emptive strikes launched against Indian airfields in the west. Twelve Sabres attacked Srinagar and four Pathankot, while Amritsar was attacked by four Mirage IIIs. The Mirages did the most damage, destroying 300 yards of Amritsar's runway and knocking out a radar post. Later in the day Sabres, operating in small packages, attacked airfields at Ambala, Agra, Jodhpur and Uttarlai as well as a number of other objectives. Three Sabres were shot down, all by ground fire. Shortly before midday the IAF launched a strong counter-offensive against PAF airfields and installations, mounting 500 sorties in a period of twenty-four hours; Hunters flew twelve sorties against Mauripur, near Karachi, and destroyed eight Sabres and a B-57 on the ground. In the air battles that developed on 4 December, the PAF lost three more Sabres on the western front, one over Amritsar, the second over Chakori and the third over Chhamb. The Sabre pilots, for their part, claimed five Indian aircraft: a Sukhoi Su-7 shot down by Flt Lt Irfan over Sargodha; a Hunter destroyed over Mauripur by Sqn Ldr Sajid; a Hunter claimed by Flt Lt Mujahid over Murir, and two more Hunters shot down over Peshawar, one by Wng Cdr Changezi and the other by Flt Lt Salim Beg. In the east, No 14 Squadron lost seven Sabres destroyed on the ground and three in air combat, all shot down by Hunters.

The IAF stepped up its attacks on airfields and installations on 5 December, and three more Sabres were destroyed on the ground. Another two were claimed by AA fire over Kashmir. By this time, Indian Army operations in the east were unfolding virtually without opposition from the air, as No 14 Squadron was reduced to three airworthy Sabres. The Sabres claimed no air combat successes on either the 5th or 6th December; in fact, most of the nineteen IAF aircraft shot down on these days were the victims of AA or small-arms fire, although a few were destroyed by Mirages and F-6s. On 6 December, two Sabres were lost to AA fire while attacking Indian positions in Kashmir, and on the eastern front a Hunter shot down one of No 14 Squadron's surviving Sabres over Comilla.

On 7 December, a Sabre flown by Flt Lt Bhatti accounted for a Hunter over Farilka; one Sabre was destroyed by Indian fighters over Munalia. As well as flying close support operations, PAF Sabres attacked Indian warships in the Arabian Sea. Three more Sabres were lost on the following day in a series of attacks on Indian airfields, and on the eastern front No 14 Squadron's two remaining aircraft were destroyed in a strafing attack, leaving the Indian Air Force with total air supremacy.

On 10 December, following a day of mixed operations involving close support and interdiction, the PAF flew at maximum effort in support of a major armoured offensive in the Chhamb sector. Sabres flew some thirty sorties against Indian rail communications in the Sind area, losing one aircraft in combat with a Hunter. On the credit side, Sabres flown by Wng Cdr Rabb and Flt Lt Taloot shot down two Su-7s that were attacking Indian forces in the Jaurian sector, and on 11 December two more Su-7s were destroyed over Shakargarh by Wng Cdr A.I. Bokhari and Sqn Ldr Cecil Choudhry. In addition, a CAP flight of four Sabres pounced on a luckless Mil Mi-8 helicopter over Munabao and shot it down. One Sabre was lost in air combat, and another was claimed by the airfield defences at Pathankot during a night attack.

On 12 December, the PAF mounted a strong ground attack effort in support of ground forces in the Sialkot-Shakargarh sector, attacking Indian armour and airfields. Three Sabres were shot down, all by ground fire. On the following day two Sabres were destroyed in the course of an air battle with Su-7s and MiG-21s which were attacking the radar station at Badin, and a third Sabre was lost to ground fire in a strafing run over Jamnagar airfield. Both air forces flew intensively in support of troops and armour locked in bitter fighting in the Shakargarh salient on 14 December, a Krishak army observation aircraft falling victim to a Sabre flown by Sqn Ldr Salim Ganhar after several minutes of desperate manoeuvring at ground level. Six Sabres attacking Srinagar airfield were intercepted by two Gnats, which had the advantage of surprise and destroyed two of the F-86s. One of the Gnats was shot down by Flt Lt Salim Baig. During another air combat over Rajasthar, a Hindustan HF-24 Marut ground attack aircraft also shot down a Sabre.

Sabres and MiG-19s continued to attack Indian armoured concentrations in the Shakargarh salient on 15 December. These sorties were strongly opposed by IAF Hunters, which shot down a Sabre and a MiG-19, while a Hunter was destroyed by an F-86 flown by Flt Lt Qari. On the next day, Sabres carried out bombing and strafing attacks on Srinagar and Avantipur airfields without loss, and on 17 December, the final day of the conflict, a Sabre flown by Flt Lt Maqsood Amir destroyed a MiG-21 over Pasrur.

The figures add up to forty-nine Sabres lost in the brief but savage war of 1971, of which fifteen were destroyed on the ground, but to this day the total remains in dispute. The PAF admitted the loss of thirty-four aircraft of all types (which would in fact correspond with the number of Sabres claimed by the Indians in air combat or during ground-attack sorties) and asserted that fifty-nine Sabres remained in service at the war's end. It should not be forgotten, however, that as well as the first-line Sabre Mk 6s, numbers of the older F-86Fs were still in use in the fighter training role, and these may have been included in the overall total.

Whatever the true facts, the PAF's Sabres

were soon replaced in first-line service by the Shenyang F-6, 140 of which eventually equipped seven squadrons. Nos 15 and 16 Squadrons continued to operate the Sabre Mk 6 in the combat training role at Chaklala until the late 1970s, when they were at last phased out. The Sabre's combat days were over.

Chapter 13
The Last of the Sabres

F-86H

While the Korean War was still in progress, North American set about developing a more powerful fighter-bomber derivative of the F-86F, intended primarily for low-level attack and differing basically from its predecessors in having a 9,300 lb s.t. General Electric J-73-GE-3 turbojet providing more than 50 per cent increase in thrust. The new variant was designated F-86H.

To accommodate the larger and more powerful engine, the basic Sabre airframe was extensively strengthened and, as the air intake duct sizes had already reached an upper limit for the size of the airframe, North American's engineers tackled the problem in much the same way Commonwealth Aviation had done when installing the Rolls-Royce Avon in the Australian-built CA-27 Sabre. They enlarged the air intake and split the fuselage lengthwise along a theoretical waterline, splicing in an extra six inches of fuselage depth. Other modifications included the provision of a clamshell-type cockpit canopy, a larger, power-boosted tailplane without dihedral, a heavier undercarriage, and improved suspension and release mechanism for underwing

The second prototype YF-86H, 52-1976, seen at Edwards AFB.

The flying shots, on this and the following pages, of the F-86H illustrate the differences between it and earlier F-86 models, notably the deeper fuselage.

ordnance loads. Fuselage fuel tanks were also fitted to supplement the normal wing tankage, so retaining the F-86F's combat radius of around 630 miles despite increased fuel consumption.

The first of two YF-86H prototypes (serial numbers 52-1975 and 52-1976) flew for the first time at Edwards AFB on 30 April 1953, with North American test pilot Joseph Lynch at the controls, and the first production F-86H-1-NH was flown four months later, on 4 September 1953. The F-86H-1-NH carried the same six .50 in. calibre machine-gun armament as earlier Sabre models, but the F-86H-5-NH and subsequent production batches carried an armament of four 20 mm M-39 cannon. Some 450 F-86H Sabres were delivered to the USAF, and were still serving with the Air National Guard in the mid-1960s.

There was no doubt that the F-86H Sabre was an exceedingly powerful aircraft in comparison with earlier versions, as was demonstrated in climb comparison tests at

Nellis Air Force Base between the F-86H and F-86F. Both aircraft were put into maximum climb simultaneously, the F-86H starting at 3,000 feet and the F-86F at 20,000 feet. At 38,000 feet the F-86H overtook the F-86F, and by the time the latter had reached 39,000 feet the F-86H had attained 40,000 feet. With both aircraft climbing from sea level, the F-86H climbed to 37,000 feet in the time it took for the F-86F to reach 19,000 feet. The F-86H's low-level performance was illustrated in 1954, when it established two speed records, achieving 649.302 mph over a 500 km closed circuit and 692.832 mph over a 100 km course.

The TF-86 Sabre Trainer
The TF-86F two-seat transonic trainer was developed from the basic F-86F in an attempt to bridge the gap between the subsonic Lockheed T-33A and the single-seat Sabre fighter. In order to accommodate the second cockpit, the fuselage was lengthened by 5 ft 3in, the wing being

The unsuccessful TF-86F two-seat trainer. Aircraft shown is the first prototype, 52-5016, which was destroyed on an early demonstration flight. Note the clamshell-type cockpit canopy.

The second TF-86F, 53-1228, was fitted with two 0.50-in guns for armament practice.

moved forward eight inches. The first of two TF-86Fs (serial 52-5016) was flown on 14 December, 1953, but failed to recover from a roll during an early demonstration flight and was destroyed. The second TF-86F (53-1228) was flown on 17 August 1954 and embodied a number of modifications, including a dorsal fin to increase airflow over the rudder for handling at low speed and high angles of attack. The aircraft was fitted with two 0.50 in machine-guns for gunnery practice. The aircraft had a loaded weight of 14,836 lb (clean) and 17,790 lb with two 166.5 Imp gall. underwing tanks.

Initial rate of climb was 10,300 ft/min and service ceiling was 50,500 ft. Maximum speed under the power of the J47-GE-27 turbojet was 611 mph at sea level. The TF-86F did not enter production.

Other Sabre Designations
The designation F-86G was originally applied to the F-86D-20-NA when it was proposed to install the J47-GE-33 engine in this aircraft; the designation F-86I was never allocated, and the designation F-86J was briefly applied to the Canadair-built Sabre Mk 6 by the USAF.

Chapter 14
FJ Fury: the Navy's Sabre

ON 27 NOVEMBER 1946, the North American XFJ-1 – the naval jet fighter whose genesis had been shared with the original XP-86 – flew for the first time under the power of a General Electric J35-GE-2 turbojet rated at 3,820 lb s.t. The performance of this very conventional aircraft soon vindicated the decision to adopt swept flying surfaces for the land-based version. Maximum speed was 533 mph at sea level and 542 mph at 16,000 feet; initial rate of climb was 4,690 ft/min, and operational ceiling 47,400 feet. The XFJ-1's range was 858 miles on its internal fuel capacity of 387 Imp gal, and this could be extended to 1,393 miles with the addition of wingtip tanks, each holding 141.5 Imp gal.

Although the XP-86 handsomely exceeded all these performance values with the exception of range, the XFJ-1 was to prove of great value to the US Navy. Despite its shortcomings, it was by far the highest-performance aircraft to serve to date in the naval fighter role, being capable of attaining 0.87 Mach in a dive.

The 1945 order for 100 production FJ-1s was reduced to thirty machines, and the first of these – now named the Fury – was delivered to Navy Fighter Squadron VF-51 at San Diego, California, late in 1947. Production aircraft differed from the three XFJ-1 prototypes in having an Allison-built J35-A-4 turbojet rated at 4,000 lb s.t.; gross wing area was also increased by the provision of wing root leading edge extensions.

On 29 February 1948, three records were broken by FJ-1 Furies. One aircraft covered the 1,025 miles from Seattle to Los Angeles in 1 hour 58 min 7 sec at an average speed of 521 mph; the second flew the 1,135 miles from Seattle to San Diego in 2 hr 12 min and 54 sec at an average speed of 511.8 mph; and the third flew from Seattle to San Francisco, a distance of 690 miles, in 1 hr 24 min, at an average speed of 492.6 mph.

On 10 March 1948, the FJ-1 underwent carrier compatibility trials aboard the USS *Boxer*, with a number of landings and take-offs carried out by Cdr Evan Aurand and Lt- Cdr R.M. Elder of VF-5A, and in the next five days all the squadron's pilots had qualified in jet aircraft operation from the carrier.

Although the FJ-1 Fury was the US Navy's first operational jet fighter, it was not the first American jet aircraft to be designed for aircraft carrier operation from the outset. That distinction went to the McDonnell XFD-1, a design that had originated in 1943. The prototype XFD-1 flew for the first time on 25 January 1945, powered by two Westinghouse J30 turbojets. On 21 July 1946 a pre-series FD-1 (series aircraft were designated FH-1) carried out the first US jet aircraft carrier trials, and as a result of these a production order for 100 aircraft – later reduced to sixty – was placed. On 15 May 1948 Fighter Squadron 17A, equipped with sixteen FH-1 Phantoms, became the first fully operational US Navy jet fighter squadron at sea, forming part of the USS *Saipan*'s air Wing.

The XFJ-1 Fury was also beaten into the air by another naval jet fighter prototype, the Chance Vought XF6U-1; the first of three prototypes flew on 2 October 1946, seven weeks before the North American aircraft. The XF6U-1 was powered by a 3,000 lb s.t. Westinghouse J34-WE-22 turbojet, later replaced by the 4,200 lb s.t. J34-WE-30A. Thirty production F6U-1s were

North American FJ-1 Fury of the US Naval Air Reserve, NAS Oakland, 1950. Many naval aviators had their first jet experience on the few FJ-1s.

ordered, but the first of these did not fly until July 1949, by which time the FJ-1 Fury had already been in service for eighteen months. The F6U-1, named the Pirate, could reach a maximum speed of 555 mph and had a range of 1,000 miles with external fuel tanks. Like the FH-1, it carried an armament of four 20 mm cannon, whereas the FJ-1 retained six 0.50 in machine-guns.

In May 1951, the FJ-1s serving with VF-5A were withdrawn from first-line service and assigned to Reserve units. In the same month the US Navy received the first examples of a much more advanced jet fighter-bomber, the Grumman F9F Panther. This type stemmed from a 1946 US Navy requirement for a shipborne night-fighter, the XF9F-1, but in October of that year the Bureau of Aeronautics elected to abandon development of this aircraft in favour of a single-engined naval day fighter, which was to be designated XF9F-2 and powered by a Rolls-Royce Nene turbojet. The first of two prototypes flew on 24 November 1947. Production aircraft

carried an armament of four 20 mm cannon and were fitted with underwing hardpoints for rockets and bombs. The first unit to equip with the Panther, in May 1951, was Fighter Squadron VF-51.

The F9F-2 Panthers of the US Navy and US Marine Corps were to give excellent service in the ground-attack role during the Korean War; so, too, was the second new type to enter service with the USN in 1949, the McDonnell F2H Banshee.

Of the two, the Panther had the higher performance. Its ultimate version, the F9F-5, was powered by the 6,250 lb s.t. Pratt & Whitney J48-P-4 turbojet, based on the Rolls-Royce Tay, and with this it reached a maximum sea level speed of 625 mph, becoming the first US Navy fighter to pass the 600 mph mark in its operational guise.

Unlike the Banshee, whose design was based in part on the earlier FH-1 Phantom, the Panther had considerable development potential, and in 1950 the Grumman design team set about enhancing the aircraft's performance by fitting the F9F-5 basic airframe with flying surfaces swept at 35 degrees. Designated XF9F-6, the prototype flew on 20 September 1951. The type was named the Cougar; the initial production batch was fitted with the 6,250 lb s.t. Pratt & Whitney J48-P-6A turbojet, but this was later replaced by the 7,250 lb s.t. J48-P-8. With this engine, the Cougar attained a maximum speed at sea level of just over 700 mph. Designated F9F-8, the Cougar entered service with Navy Fighter Squadron VF-32 in November 1952.

Meanwhile, events in Korea had shown that neither the Panther nor the Banshee could operate in MiG-dominated airspace without suffering unacceptable losses, and the US Navy, in the knowledge that it was possible to operate swept-wing fighters from aircraft carriers, had become interested in a North American design proposal for a navalized version of the F-86E Sabre, the NA-181. On 10 February 1951, the

Bureau of Aeronautics issued a letter of contract for the development of prototypes, and Commander Evan Aurand, who had carried out the original deck landing trials with the FJ-1 Fury, was appointed Navy Project Officer.

The first two prototypes, 133754 and 133755, were F-86E airframes fitted with essential equipment for carrier operations; a catapult spool in the belly and an A-frame type arrester hook which faired absolutely flush under the rear fuselage. They were also fitted with lengthened nose oleos to compensate for the high angle of attack required for a catapult launch.

The third prototype, 133756, was fully navalized, having folding wings in addition to the other equipment, and was the first to carry the full armament of four 20 mm Mk-12 cannon, a change demanded by the Navy in place of the Sabre's six machine-guns. Designated XFJ-2B, this aircraft was in fact the first to fly, test pilot

An FJ-2 Fury caught at the instant of being catapulted from the deck of the USS *Coral Sea*. The machine is the first prototype, assigned to the Naval Air Test Center, Patuxent River.

The second prototype FJ-2 Fury, 133756, in flight off the coast of California.

FJ-2 Fury in US Marine Corps markings. All the FJ-2 production went to the USMC.

Robert Hoover taking it on its maiden flight on 27 December 1951.

The two modified F-86Es, designated XFJ-2s, were delivered to the US Navy Test Center at Patuxent River early in 1952, while the XFJ-2B went to the Ordnance Test Station, Inyokern, for armament trials. The US Navy officially accepted the three prototypes in June, July and December respectively, and carrier qualification trials were completed aboard the USS *Coral Sea* in December 1952. These followed earlier evaluation, in August 1952, on the USS *Midway*.

The US Navy had already placed an order for 300 production FJ-2s on 10 February 1951, and construction of these aircraft was initiated at North American's new factory in Columbus, Ohio. With the running-down of the war in Korea, the order was later decreased to 200 aircraft, serials 131927 to 132126. The first production FJ-2 Fury was accepted by the US Navy in October 1952 and production continued until September 1954.

The FJ-2 Fury was in effect the US Navy equivalent of the F-86F, and had all the features that characterized that mark. It was powered by a 6,000 lb s.t. General Electric J47-GE-2, the naval version of the J47-GE-27. The addition of the necessary naval equipment raised the take-off weight to 18,791 lb compared to the F-86F's 17,797 lb. Maximum speed was 676 mph at sea level, and 602 mph at 36,000 ft. The four 20 mm cannon, which carried 150 rounds per gun, were aimed by a Mk 16 Model 2 sight and AN/APG-30 radar.

Because most of the production line at the Columbus plant was involved with the F-86F during 1952, work on the FJ-2 proceeded slowly, and only five aircraft had been completed by the end of the year. In fact, it was not until January 1954 that the first FJ-2 was delivered to an operational unit: this was Marine Squadron VMF-122 at

FJ-3 Fury of Navy Fighter Squadron VF-33. The FJ-3, equivalent to the F-86H Sabre, shows the latter's deeper fuselage contours.

Cherry Point, North Carolina. Because the US Navy preferred the F9F-8 Cougar, which had a better deck performance, the whole FJ-2 production went to the Marine Corps, and by 1955 the Fury equipped six USMC squadrons: VMF-122, 232 and 312 with the Atlantic Fleet, and VMF-235, 334 and 451 with the Pacific Fleet.

It was VMF-235 which, in June 1954, carried out operational trials with its FJ-2s aboard the USS *Hancock*, the first US carrier to be fitted with the British-developed steam catapult. In the course of the month, 254 launchings were made by FJ-2s and a variety of other naval aircraft.

Meanwhile, in March 1952, North American – aware of the FJ-2's shortcomings, and alarmed by the failure to secure a prime US Navy production contract – had begun work on an uprated version of the aircraft, the FJ-3. This was powered by a 7,700 lb thrust Wright J65-W-2 engine, the licence-built version of the Armstrong Siddeley Sapphire; the engine was tested in the fifth production FJ-2, 131931.

There was no XFJ-3, and the first production FJ-3 was completed at Columbus on 11 December 1953, being flown on the same day. Production orders for the new variant totalled 389 (serials 135774 to 136162), and this time the bulk went to the US Navy. Apart from the different engine, the FJ-3 had a larger air intake than the FJ-2, reminiscent of the F-86H Sabre, and ammunition for the 20 mm guns was increased by forty-eight rounds.

By July 1954, twenty-four FJ-3s had been accepted by the US Navy; these equipped VX-3 and VF-173, which carried out the Fleet Introduction Programme at Patuxent River in the record time of twenty-nine days, completing 703 flying hours. Two aircraft were lost during this period, one when its engine blew up after sustaining foreign object damage and the other when it ran out of fuel and ditched in the Patuxent River after its pilot got lost.

On 8 May 1955, VF-173 flew its FJ-3s out

into the Atlantic to join the carrier USS *Bennington*, and on 22 August that year VX-3 began operational evaluation of the mirror landing system installed in this vessel, the first landing being made by VX-3's commanding officer, Cdr R.G. Dose. (The first night landing using the mirror system was made two days later by Lt-Cdr H.C. MacKnight, in a F9F-8 Cougar.) Another Fury 'first' came in January 1956, when aircraft of VF-21 landed on the USS *Forrestal*, the first carrier designed and built specifically for jet aircraft operation.

During 1955 the FJ-3 Fury had undergone a number of modifications. Wing slats were replaced by extended leading edges which housed an extra 124 gallons of fuel, and underwing stores points were increased from two to six, enabling the aircraft to carry 500- or 1,000-lb bombs, rocket packs or additional fuel tanks. Sidewinder air-to-air missiles, first tested in 1952, were fitted on the Fury from the 345th aircraft onwards, and Furies so equipped were designated FJ-3M. The initial overseas deployment of a Sidewinder-equipped missile unit took place on 14 July 1956, when VA-46, equipped with F9F-8 Cougars, departed from Norfolk, Virginia, on the USS *Randolph* for operations with the Sixth Fleet in the Mediterranean; in the following month, deployment of the Sidewinder was extended to the Western Pacific when VF-211 sailed with its Furies on the USS *Bon Homme Richard* for operations with the Seventh Fleet.

By August 1956, the FJ-3/3M Fury formed the equipment of twenty-three US Navy and Marine Corps squadrons. Serving with the Atlantic Fleet were VA-172, VF-12, VF-33, VF-62, VF-73, VF-84, VF-173, VMF-122, VMF-312 and VMF-334, while VF-21, VF-24, VF-51, VF-91, VF-121, VF-142, VF-143, VF-191, VF-211 and VMF-235 were on station in the Pacific. VX-3, the trials unit, was shore-based, together with Marine Corps Squadrons VMF-333 and VMF-511.

On 1 September 1956, four FJ-3 Furies of VF-24 competed for the North American

The ultimate Fury, the FJ-4B. Note the six rocket packs and the in-flight refuelling probe.

Trophy, taking off from the USS *Shangri-La* at sea off the Pacific coast of Mexico and flying 1,198 miles to Oklahoma city nonstop. The winner was Lt (jg) D.K. Grosshuesch, with a time of 2 hours 13 minutes 38.6 seconds at an average speed of 537.848 mph.

The FJ-3 Fury was the last of the line to bear a close family resemblance to its progenitor, the Sabre. The next variant, the FJ-4, was so much altered in design that it was virtually a new type. Design of the FJ-4, which was classified as a long-range attack fighter, was started at the Columbus plant in February 1953, and in June that year the project was placed on a firm basis with an order for two prototypes under the Company designation NA-208.

Meeting the primary requirement of extended range meant increasing the Fury's fuel capacity by 50 per cent, which in turn meant a revision of the entire airframe to compensate for a substantial increase in gross weight. For the first time, the wing platform departed from that common to all previous Sabres and Furies. The FJ-4's wing was thinner, using integral skin/stringers and multi-spar construction, and was milled from solid aluminium plate. Span and area were increased and mid-span control surfaces and high-lift flaps were incorporated. The tail surfaces were also thinner, and incorporated mid-span controls. Because of its attack role, the FJ-4 featured extra armour in the nose, the amount of 20 mm ammunition being reduced by way of compensation. The aircraft was fitted with a new levered-suspension undercarriage, increasing the track to 11 ft 7 in. The fuselage and cockpit contours were revised, the fuselage being deeper than that of the FJ-3 embodying a prominent dorsal spine.

The first of the two FJ-4 prototypes (serials 139279 and 138280) was flown by test pilot Richard Wenzell on 28 October 1954. This aircraft was powered by the FJ-3's Wright J65-W-4, but production aircraft were fitted with the 7,700 lb thrust J65-W-16A. The FJ-4 had four underwing stores

stations, and performance included a maximum speed of 680 mph at sea level and 630 mph at 36,000 ft.

Under the Company designation NA-209, 150 production FJ-4s were ordered on 16 October 1953, the first of these being delivered to USMC Squadron VMF-451 with the Pacific Fleet at the end of 1956. On 4 December that year a new variant, the FJ-4B, made its first flight; this had a strengthened wing to accommodate six underwing stores positions and was nuclear-capable, being fitted with a Low Altitude Bombing System (LABS) for the delivery of a tactical atomic weapon. Additional speed brakes were also fitted under the rear fuselage to provide better control at low level.

All the USMC's FJ-4 Furies served with Pacific Fleet units. VMF-232, 235 and 451 used the earlier model, while the FJ-4B equipped VMA-212, 214 and 223. The -4B also served with ten US Navy Pacific Fleet squadrons: VA-55, 56, 63, 116, 126, 146, 151, 192, 212 and 216.

The Fleet Introduction Programme of the FJ-4B was undertaken by VA-126 and VMA-223, with particular emphasis on low-level nuclear weapons delivery. The FJ-4B had a flight refuelling probe installed in the port wing, and from June 1957 underwing fuel packs came into use under the so-called 'Buddy-Buddy' in-flight refuelling system, enabling a Fury to take on an additional 3,163 lb of fuel from an aircraft of the same type. In October 1958, F-4Js of VMA-212 and VMA-214 completed the first trans-Pacific crossing by single-seat naval aircraft, flying from MCAS Kaneohe to NAS Atsugi, Japan, with stopovers at Midway and Guam. Designated Operation *Cannonball*, the flight – involving twenty-four aircraft in two sections – rendezvoused with USAF Boeing KB-50 tankers off Wake Island, and with North American AJ-1 Savage aircraft near Iwo Jima.

On 25 April 1959, the FJ-4Bs of VA-212 became the first to deploy overseas with the Martin Bullpup precision air-to-surface missile, sailing from Alameda on board the USS *Lexington* to join the Seventh Fleet in the western Pacific. The Fury could carry five Bullpups, plus the associated equipment pack.

By 1960, the Fury was being phased out of first-line service and allocated to Reserve units, where it was to continue for some years longer. The last first-line squadron to use it, until September 1962, was VA-126. In all, 1,115 Furies of all marks were delivered between January 1952, when the first XFJ-2 went to Patuxent River for evaluation, and May 1958.

Unlike the F-86 Sabre from which it was derived, the FJ Fury never saw combat. Yet it formed a principal combat component of the US Navy and Marine Corps during a dangerous and unstable period, particularly in the Pacific, where there was armed confrontation between Communist and Nationalist China during the late 1950s. If the United States had become involved in an escalating war in that area, its carrier forces would have been at the forefront of it; and there is little doubt that the Fury would have given an excellent account of itself.

Chapter 15
The F-100 Super Sabre

ALTHOUGH IT emerged as a completely different design, the North American F-100 Super Sabre merits inclusion in this work because it stemmed directly from the basic F-86 concept.

The evolution of the Super Sabre began on 3 February 1949, when Raymond H. Rice and the North American design team began preliminary studies of an advanced version of the latest mark of Sabre, the F-86D, with a view to producing an aircraft capable of reaching and sustaining supersonic speeds in level flight. There was no longer any doubt that this goal was perfectly feasible; high-speed research by rocket-powered aircraft such as the Bell X-

1 was constantly adding to the available data, and the F-86 itself had proved that the transition from subsonic to supersonic flight presented no aerodynamic problems, even though the Sabre's incursions into the supersonic realm were, of necessity, very brief.

The first and most important task was to reduce supersonic drag, and North American hoped to achieve a reduction of about fifty per cent – compared to existing swept-wing designs – by combining a wing swept at 45 degrees with a contoured fuselage. By September 1949 the design of the aircraft, known to the Company as the Sabre 45, was advanced enough for a proposal to be laid before the USAF.

The first production F-100A Super Sabre, 52-5756.

128

Close-up of the F-100's air intake and the long pitot tube, designed to keep the pitot head clear of sonic shock waves.

Reaction at first was slow, but the appearance of the MiG-15 over Korea late in 1950 gave the necessary impetus to the idea, and in January 1951 North American were sufficiently encouraged by the USAF's interest to begin more detailed work on the project. On 1 November, the Company received a USAF contract for the building of two prototypes, designated YF-100A, and 110 production F-100A fighters.

It is interesting, at this point, to make a comparison between supersonic fighter development in the United States and on the other side of the Atlantic. In November 1951 – the very month in which North American was awarded the F-100 contract

– Hawker Aircraft Ltd of Great Britain began detailed design work on a project designated P.1083; this was in effect a supersonic version of the Hawker Hunter, the prototype of which had flown in the previous July. The P.1083 was a straightforward development of the Hunter, featuring a lengthened fuselage to accommodate an afterburning Rolls-Royce Avon RA.19 turbojet and married to a new thin wing, swept 52 degrees at the leading edge and with a thickness/chord ratio of only 7.5 degrees.

Performance estimates for the P.1083, at a loaded weight of 17,700 lb with half fuel, included a maximum speed of 820 mph

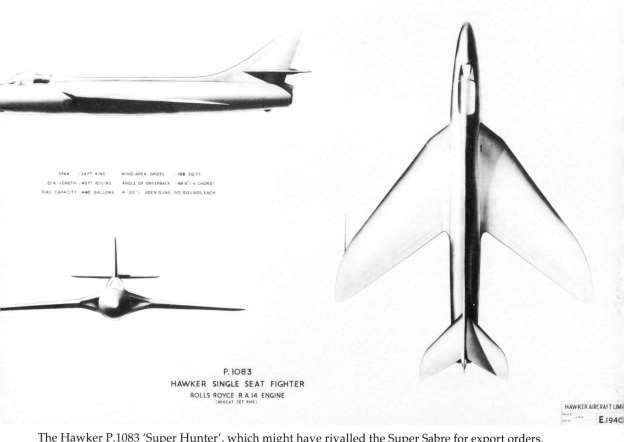

SPAN - 34 FT. 4 INS.   WING AREA GROSS - 358 SQ.FT.
O/A LENGTH - 45 FT. 10½ INS.   ANGLE OF SWEEPBACK - 48-E° (¼ CHORD)
FUEL CAPACITY - 440 GALLONS.   4 - 30"- ADEN GUNS 150 ROUNDS EACH

P. 1083
HAWKER SINGLE SEAT FIGHTER
ROLLS ROYCE R.A.14 ENGINE
(REHEAT JET PIPE)

HAWKER AIRCRAFT LIM

E.194C

The Hawker P.1083 'Super Hunter', which might have rivalled the Super Sabre for export orders.

(1.248M) at sea level, 790 mph (1.2M) at 36,000 ft, and 690 mph (1.05M) at 55,000 ft. Estimated initial rate of climb was 50,000 ft/min at sea level, 28,700 ft/min at 20,000 ft, and 5,400 ft/min at 50,000 ft. Estimated service ceiling was 59,500 ft, while time to 30,000 ft at an all-up weight of 20,000 lb was estimated to be one minute fifty-seven seconds, and to 55,000 ft five minutes twelve seconds from the start of the take-off roll.

There is no reason at all to doubt the accuracy of these estimates. Neither is there any doubt that the performance of the lighter, more manoeuvrable P.1083, the so-called 'Super Hunter', would have been superior in most respects to that of the F-100, particularly in time-to-altitude. But in July 1953, with the prototype 80 per cent complete, the RAF Air Staff turned aside from the use of afterburning engines like the RA.19 and the P.1083 was cancelled. The RAF would not have a supersonic fighter until 1960, when the English Electric Lightning entered service.

The decision to cancel the P.1083 had a considerable impact on Britain's future military export market. Apart from Britain, no fewer than sixteen other countries went on to use the Hawker Hunter; and when some of them, particularly those in NATO, came to look for a supersonic successor in the late 1950s, they chose the F-100 because Britain had nothing to offer them.

The F-100 mockup was approved by the USAF on 26 August 1952, and the first YF-100A prototype (52-5754) was completed on 24 April 1953 and secretly moved to Edwards AFB for flight testing. The aircraft was powered by a Pratt & Whitney J57-P-7 two-stage turbojet rated at 9,700 lb thrust (14,800 lb with afterburner). On 25 May, North American chief test pilot George Welch – who had first flown the F-86 – took the YF-100A on its maiden flight, during which he effortlessly exceeded Mach One.

By 15 September 1953 the YF-100A had made thirty-nine test flights, totalling nineteen hours and forty-two minutes, and the USAF Phase II test programme had been completed. On 20 October the aircraft was shown to the public for the first time, the Press reporting that the sonic booms from its low-level supersonic dives 'left onlookers gasping and children crying', and nine days later, flown by Lt-Col F.K. Everest, chief of test operations at Edwards AFB, it set a new world air speed record of 755.149 mph over a fifteen-kilometre course. The previous record, set by a Douglas A4D-1 Skyray, was 753.4 mph.

On the same day – 29 October 1953 – George Welch made the first flight of a production F-100A, 52-5756. This aircraft carried four M-39 guns with 800 rounds of ammunition. Tested in Korea by modified F-86Fs, the M-39 had a rate of fire of 1,500 rounds per minute. A radar ranging device was installed in the upper lip of the F-100's nose inlet.

Designed as a straightforward air superiority fighter, the F-100A was intended to replace the F-86 Sabre in this role, and its method of operation was much the same as the earlier aircraft's. It would take off with two 275-gallon tanks at a gross weight of 28,899 lb, fly out to a combat radius of about 350 miles, and jettison its tanks before combat. At a combat weight of 24,996 lb, with sixty per cent fuel, it had a speed range of 760 mph (1.0M) at sea level to 825 mph (1.285M) at 35,000 ft. Operational ceiling was 51,000 ft.

Testing of the F-100 proceeded remarkably smoothly; production was on schedule and the USAF looked forward to the early re-equipment of its day fighter force, which at that time comprised twelve F-84F, thirteen F-86F and the three F-86H wings. The first Tactical Air Command unit to receive the Super Sabre, in September 1954, was the 479th Fighter Day Wing at George Air Force Base, in the high desert country of California. By this time, however, it was apparent that all was not well with the F-100. North American Aviation was receiving disturbing reports from USAF pilots who had been having stability and control problems with the aircraft. The trouble seemed to lie with the F-100A's vertical tail, which was smaller than that of the YF-100A and which did not appear large enough to maintain adequate directional stability.

The half-expected tragedy came on 12 October 1954, when George Welch took 52-5674 high over the Mojave desert for a supersonic dive from 45,000 ft, followed by a maximum-G pullup. The F-100A broke up in the dive; Welch baled out, but was fatally injured by flying debris. In the month that followed there were five more major accidents, one involving a senior Royal Air Force officer, Air Commodore G.D. Stephenson, who was killed at Eglin AFB when his F-100A went out of control. On 10 November, the USAF grounded the entire Super Sabre fleet pending investigations.

Welch's aircraft had been heavily instrumented, and it was a five-inch piece of film salvaged from the wreckage that provided the clue. It showed the shadow of the fin, moving across the tailplane. The aircraft had begun to yaw while still at a high Mach number. The yawing motion had increased to the point where the vertical tail could no longer compensate for it. The F-100A had gone suddenly and wildly out of control and had been literally torn apart by the supersonic airstream.

North American's answer to the problem

F-100As of the 479th Day Fighter Wing, George AFB, California, the first Tactical Air Command unit to equip with the aircraft.

was to increase the F-100A's vertical tail area by twenty-seven per cent to delay the onset of instability above 1.4M. The wingtips were also extended to increase span and wing area, and the artificial feel systems for the aileron and stabilizer powered controls were modified. With these modifications the F-100A was returned to service after three months, and in September 1955 the 479th Fighter Wing achieved initial operational capability (IOC) with the new type. By this time, a total of 203 F-100As had been accepted by the USAF.

The F-100A was phased out of first-line USAF service from 1958. Despite its high performance, it had failed for a variety of reasons to meet the air superiority fighter criterion demanded of it. Aircraft were assigned to the Air National Guard or placed in storage, with the exception of fifteen examples which were sent to Nationalist China, which ultimately received 118. Some ANG F-100As were returned to active duty at the time of the Berlin crisis of 1961.

Early in 1953, in response to a USAF request, North American's engineers had indicated that it would be feasible to build fuel tanks into the F-100's wings in order to extend the combat radius, and later in the year they also affirmed that the wing structure could be strengthened to carry external stores. This was a recipe for a fighter-bomber, an aircraft the USAF badly needed, and on 30 December 1953 North American were instructed that the last 70 aircraft of the F-100A contract should be produced as air superiority fighters with a fighter-bomber capability, the revised version being designated F-100C. A further contract, issued on 24 February 1954, authorized production of an additional 230 examples of this model.

The F-100C flew for the first time on 17 January 1955 and deliveries to USAF Tactical Air Command began in April, the aircraft becoming operational with the 450th Squadron of the 322nd Fighter Day Group at Foster AFB, Texas, on 14 July. Further orders had meanwhile raised the total of F-100Cs to 476, the last being delivered in July 1956. About one-third of the F-100Cs on the USAF inventory were deployed with the United States Air Forces Europe (USAFE).

For its fighter-bomber role, the F-100C had six underwing stations for 750 lb bombs or other stores up to a maximum of 5,000 lb. The largest store that it could carry was the 2,000 lb Mk-7 'special' (ie nuclear) weapon, which was released by an MA-2 low-altitude bombing system. In addition to its built-in armament of four 20 mm M-39 guns, the F-100C could carry forty-two 2.75 in folding-fin aircraft rockets (FFAR) in two packs. Thanks to the 'wet' wing, fuel capacity was raised from 744 gallons in the F-100A to 1,702 gallons, and an in-flight refuelling system was added, enabling the F-100C to perform the dual role of fighter-bomber and fighter-escort on long-range penetration missions.

The F-100C was a step in the right direction, but although it received a number of modifications during its in-service life – such as provision for Sidewinder AAMs and the carriage of cluster bomb units – it was clear that much more improvement was needed if it was to discharge its role adequately.

North America's answer, first flown on 24 January 1956, was the F-100D, which was developed as a dedicated fighter-bomber. This model featured a slight increase in vertical tail area and was equipped with a Minneapolis-Honeywell MB-3 automatic pilot, the first developed for a supersonic jet, which was intended to allow the pilot to concentrate on navigation or tactics while the aircraft flew itself to the target. Improved electronic LABS equipment was fitted for the delivery of Mk-7, Mk-38 or Mk-43 nuclear stores, and provision was made for the carriage of two 450 gallon external fuel tanks for air-to-air refuelling. Conventional weapons loads included six 750 lb or four 1,000 lb bombs, or two GAM-83A air-to-surface missiles. For self defence, the F-100D could carry four GAR-8 Sidewinder AAMs, provision for these being made about halfway through the production run.

The first F-100Ds were delivered to the 405th Fighter-Bomber Wing at Langley AFB, Virginia, in September 1956. North American built 940 F-100Ds in Los Angeles and 334 in Columbus. The last 148 production aircraft had built-in zero-length launch capability; this technique, the subject of many trials by the USAF in the 1950s, enabled tactical aircraft like the F-100 to be rocket-launched from an angled ramp.

Although USAF pilots had found it relatively easy to make the jump from the Lockheed T-33A trainer to the F-86 Sabre, the transition from F-86 or F-84F to the F-100 proved far more difficult, and the type had a deplorable in-service accident rate; for example, fifty F-100As – one-quarter of the total number delivered – were lost in accidents.

To remedy matters, on 10 May 1954 North American Aviation began design studies of a supersonic trainer, and on 2 September submitted the proposal to the USAF, offering to modify a standard single-seat F-100C to trainer configuration at no cost to the Air Force. It was an offer the Air Force could hardly refuse, and North American received an initial production contract for 259 TF-100Cs. The prototype (54-1966, which had been loaned to the company by the USAF) flew on 3 August 1956. It was destroyed on 9 April 1957 during demonstration spin testing, NAA chief engineering test pilot Bob Baker ejecting safely.

The production two-seaters had their designation changed to F-100F, and the first of these was flown by NAA pilot Gage Mace on 7 March 1957. In May, the first F-100F was assigned to an operational training squadron at Nellis AFB.

A special production model, the F-100F-20, was developed at the request of Pacific Air Forces. Optimized for overwater flying, this version was equipped with a navigational system that included an AN/ASN-7 dead-reckoning computer, PC-212 Doppler radar and a standard J-4 compass system. It also had modified flaps, with a duct built into the leading edges to direct air from the lower surface over the upper to reduce wing buffet during landing.

The system was subjected to intensive testing, and the subsequent report cautiously stated that if it were used correctly, it would increase the probability of reaching the target, even in adverse

F-100D Super Sabre of the 55th Sqn, 20th TFW, photographed at RAF Wethersfield on 11 June 1966. Note the wing fences.

weather, after a long run over water. But, because of the system's limitations, missions had to be flown straight and level at high altitude, which was not a recipe for survival.

In general, the two-seater F-100 was not as successful as had been hoped. In fact, its accident rate was as high as the F-100A's had been; by the time it was phased out, one-quarter of the fleet had been destroyed.

In 1964, ten F-100D Wings were in operation, together with eleven Air National Guard squadrons equipped with the F-100A and F-100C. These were, in the continental United States:

3rd Tactical Fighter Wing (90th, 416th, 510th and 531st Tactical Fighter Squadrons) at England AFB, Louisiana;
27th Tactical Fighter Wing (478th, 522nd, 523rd and 524th Tactical Fighter Squadrons) at Cannon AFB, New Mexico;
31st Tactical Fighter Wing (306th, 307th, 308th and 309th Tactical Fighter Squadrons) at Homestead AFB, Florida;
354th Tactical Fighter Wing (352nd, 353rd, 355th and 356th Tactical Fighter Squadrons) at Myrtle Beach AFB, South Carolina;
401st Tactical Fighter Wing (612th, 613th, 614th and 615th Tactical Fighter Squadrons) at England AFB, Louisiana;
474th Tactical Fighter Wing (428th, 429th, 430th and 431st Tactical Fighter Squadrons) at Cannon AFB, New Mexico.

The F-100 units deployed overseas were:

20th Tactical Fighter Wing (55th, 77th and 79th Tactical Fighter Squadrons) at Wethersfield, United Kingdom;
48th Tactical Fighter Wing (492nd, 493rd and 494th Tactical Fighter Squadrons) at Lakenheath, United Kingdom,
50th Tactical Fighter Wing (10th, 81st and 417th Tactical Fighter Squadrons) at Hahn, Germany;
405th Tactical Fighter Wing (511th Tactical

Fighter Squadron) at Clark AFB in the Philippines. (The 405th's other squadron, the 509th Tactical Fighter Squadron, was equipped with F-102 Delta Daggers.)

Squadrons of the Air National Guard equipped with the F-100 were:

152nd Fighter Interceptor Squadron at Tucson, Arizona;
188th Tactical Fighter Squadron at Albuquerque, New Mexico;
110th Tactical Fighter Squadron at St Louis, Missouri;
118th Fighter Interceptor Squadron at Hartford, Connecticut;
119th Tactical Fighter Squadron at Atlantic City, New Jersey;
120th Tactical Fighter Squadron at Denver, Colorado;
121st Tactical Fighter Squadron, District of Colombia;
127th Tactical Fighter Squadron, Wichita, Kansas;
136th Tactical Fighter Squadron, Niagara Falls, New York;
166th Tactical Fighter Squadron, Lockbourne, Ohio;
174th Tactical Fighter Squadron, Sioux City, Iowa.

Many of the 2,294 Super Sabres built found their way into foreign air forces. As well as those supplied to Nationalist China, 260 F-100Cs equipped four fighter-bomber wings of the Turkish Air Force; F-100Ds equipped Nos 725, 727, and 730 Squadrons of the Royal Danish Air Force (which had previously used Hawker Hunters!); and the type was used by the French Air Force's 3ᵉ and 11ᵉ Escadres de Chasse.

In June 1964, the Super Sabre went to war. In response to the shooting down of a US Navy F-8 Crusader over the Plain des Jarres, Laos, eight F-100Ds of the 615th Tactical Fighter Squadron, on temporary duty (TDY) at Clark AFB in the Philippines, were deployed to Da Nang, the northernmost air base in the Republic of Vietnam, and sent to attack a fortified point near where the incident had occurred. Each aircraft carried thirty-eight rockets in two pods and four 500 lb bombs. The mission was hardly a success; only a handful of bombs fell in the target area, the remainder having been dropped twenty-five miles away by the second F-100 flight. The fault lay not with the pilots, but with inadequate target intelligence, poor planning and unfamiliarity with the terrain.

In the weeks that followed, other F-100 units were rotated through Da Nang and also to Takhli, a Royal Laotian Air Force base. Initial deployments included the 27th, 401st and 405th TFS. On 18 August 1964, the F-100 force sustained its first battle damage when one of four Super Sabres on a Rescue Combat Air Patrol (RESCAP) was hit by Pathet Lao gunfire; the pilot ejected over Thailand and was picked up safely. On 18 November, another F-100 was shot down in central Laos and the pilot was killed.

In December 1964, F-100s took part in Operation *Barrel Roll*, a limited series of air strikes in Laos near the border with North Vietnam. The first mission, on 14 December, was an attack by F-105s against Route 8, the main strategic artery between Laos and North Vietnam; on this occasion the F-100s flew MiGCAP (MiG Combat Air Patrol), but on the 21st four Super Sabres of the 428th TFS made an unsuccessful attack on Route 8 with cluster munitions and 2.75 inch rockets.

On 13 January 1965 the F-100s were in action again, attacking AA sites around the Ban Ken bridge in northern Laos, the target of an F-105 strike. Eight F-100s, each carrying CBU-2A cluster bombs, attacked in line abreast at low level but failed to knock out all of the guns. One F-100 and an F-105 were shot down. On 8 February, twenty F-100s again acted in the defence suppression role, attacking gun positions at Chap Le in North Vietnam while A-1 Skyraiders bombed an adjacent military barracks. Three days later, twenty-eight more F-100s again attacked AA sites in the same area, and on 24 February F-100s of the 613th TFS

provided cover for Army helicopters evacuating South Vietnamese troops who had been surrounded in the An Khe valley in the central highlands of Vietnam.

On 2 March 1965, Operation *Rolling Thunder* began with a strike against an ammunition depot at Xom Bong, thirty-five miles inside North Vietnam. The attack was led by forty-four F-100s from Da Nang, hitting the defences with 2.75 in rockets and 20 mm cannon fire. One F-100 was hit and its pilot, Lt Hayden Lockhart, Jr, became the first USAF pilot to be captured by the enemy. Another Super Sabre was lost on 3 April on a defence suppression mission to Thanh Hoa, where F-105s were attacking a bridge. The bridge survived, and the mission was repeated on the following day. On this occasion, the strike was bounced by four MiG-17s, which dived straight through the MiGCAP of 416th TFS Super Sabres and shot down two of the Thunderchiefs. One F-100 pilot launched a Sidewinder and another engaged a MiG with cannon; both missed. The USAF learned a stark lesson that day; powerful though it was, the F-100 was inferior even to the MiG-17 in air combat. Not until the much better equipped F-4 Phantom arrived on the scene would the Americans be in a position to achieve air superiority.

Over the next two years, the F-100 force in Vietnam steadily increased, and by the middle of 1967 four tactical fighter wings were operating in the theatre; these were the 3rd, 31st, 35th and 37th TFWs. When the Air National Guard was called to active duty in 1968, each Wing gained ANG units, so that the total number of F-100s available in Vietnam – on paper at least – grew to about 480 aircraft.

Super Sabre missions were now confined to the area south of the Demilitarized Zone (DMZ) and fell into five categories. These were direct air support missions, flown against known or suspected enemy positions, facilities or routes; close air support, flown against enemy targets near friendly forces; escort missions for C-123 aircraft carrying out defoliation operations;

air cover missions for resupply transport aircraft; landing zone preparation missions, in which the F-100s delivered ordnance to suppress enemy action during the landing of friendly forces by helicopter or fixed-wing aircraft; and landing zone construction, which involved dropping blast weapons to clear a landing zone by flattening trees and vegetation.

For direct air support missions, the ordnance carried was usually a mixture of 750 lb Snakeye bombs and 750 lb canisters of napalm, or alternatively 750 lb bombs fused to detonate below ground. Close air support usually involved dropping napalm and then strafing the target with cannon; many of these missions were flown at night, the F-100s working in conjunction with flare-dropping C-47s. On daytime missions the F-100s worked with a Forward

Air Controller, usually in an OV-10 Bronco. After take-off, the Super Sabres would climb to 15–18,000 feet for transit to the target area, being directed at this stage by an airborne command, control and communications aircraft, which handed them over to the FAC as they approached the target area. Over the target, the F-100s would orbit, still at altitude, until the objective was marked, when the fighter-bombers would let down singly to 9,000 feet and start the roll-in to the target. If bounced by MiG-21s (unlikely south of the DMZ, but always a possibility) F-100 pilots were briefed to dive to ground level and go supersonic, which the MiG-21 could not do at low altitude.

In the summer of 1965, a serious new threat developed to US aircraft operating over North Vietnam: the SA-2 Guide-

The F-100F, unsuccessful as a trainer, went on to pioneer *Wild Weasel* defence suppression techniques in South-East Asia.

line surface-to-air missile. Sites began to spring up around key points all over the north, and strike aircraft began to take losses.

The SA-2's principal weakness was that it was radar-guided. If the radars were destroyed, the missile was useless. What was needed was an aircraft fitted with electronic equipment that would give warning of a missile radar in operation; the site could then be attacked by the aircraft itself, or by others accompanying it.

Lightweight, compact radar warning equipment was already available, having been developed by a small American company, Applied Technology Inc., for installation in Lockheed U-2 high-altitude reconnaissance aircraft. After investigating a number of options, a USAF committee recommended that a modified version of this equipment be installed in tactical fighter bombers, creating a specialized hunter-killer aircraft that could detect, locate and destroy the enemy missile radars. The high-priority programme was called *Wild Weasel I*.

The aircraft selected to pioneer the new role was the two-seat F-100F-20 Super Sabre, and the North American engineers at Los Angeles set about modifying six aircraft (58-1221 to 58-1226). The electronic equipment had three main functions: to warn aircrews that the aircraft was being illuminated by *Fan Song, Firecan* and other anti-aircraft and airborne interception radars, to warn that a missile was about to be launched (which it did by sensing a power change in the SA-2's L-band *Fan Song* command guidance radar), and to provide automatic direction-finding of the SAM radar signals, allowing strike aircraft to home on to them with a high degree of accuracy.

The system was tested at Los Angeles and Eglin AFB, where selected crews flew simulated combat missions of the kind that would be required in Vietnam. By the end of November, 1965, the four F-100F Wild Weasels were in position at Korat Royal Thai Air Force Base, and the first combat

mission was flown on 3 December, with two F-100Fs leading a flight of F-105Ds. Later, the usual combination was one F-100F and four F-105s; these missions went under the code-name *Iron Hand*. The usual technique was for the F-100F to mark the target with a salvo of twenty-four rockets, after which the F-105s would hit it with bombs.

It was a risky business, and on 20 December 1965 an F-100F was hit by a 37 mm AA shell during a strike north of Haiphong. Both crewmen ejected; the pilot was captured and the weapon systems operator was killed attempting to resist capture. Two days later, the Weasels had their revenge when the crew of 1226 destroyed a SAM radar system during a *Rolling Thunder* strike against rail yards at Yen Bai, northwest of Hanoi.

Three more Wild Weasel F-100Fs arrived in the theatre in February 1966, and in April they received new offensive equipment in the shape of the AGM-45A Shrike anti-radar missile, equipped with a passive homing system that directed it to ride an enemy radar beam down to its source. The first combat mission with this weapon was flown on 18 April 1966, when an F-100F and three F-105s attacked a *Fire Can*-towed, trailer-mounted tracking radar used with 57 mm and 85 mm AAA. A Shrike was launched, but visibility was poor and there was no confirmed result.

From mid-1966, the Wild Weasel role in Vietnam was assumed by the F-105 and the F-4, the surviving F-100Fs (two having been lost in action) returning to the United States. The Wild Weasel Is had laboured under a great many frustrations; their stop-gap aircraft had not really been suited to the task, and their electronic equipment had been subjected to frequent malfunctions. Nevertheless, they had pioneered a new role – one that was to assume tremendous importance in the hostile electronic environment of modern war.

The F-100F played another important part in the Vietnam War, too – that of Forward Air Controller. By mid-1966,

FACs flying piston-engined aircraft just north of the DMZ were suffering unacceptable losses to ground fire, and so the USAF hit upon the idea of putting a FAC in the back seat of a fast jet, either an F-100F or an F-4. In 1967, under the code-name *Commando Sabre*, the mission was assigned to the 612th Tactical Fighter Squadron's Detachment 1, attached to the 37th TFW at Phu Cat. Later, the 612th became a headquarters squadron, attached to the 31st TFW at Tuy Hoa and operating F-100Fs drawn from other units at that base. After a number of trial missions, the high-speed FAC became standard where there were SAMs, AAA and a threat of MiGs. When the F-100F crew located a worthwhile target, they would pass its co-ordinates to an airborne command post, which would call in a strike of F-4s, F-100Ds or F-105s. The strike aircraft would call visual contact with the F-100F, which would then mark the target – often a truck park – with white phosphorus rockets. These missions were popularly called 'Misty FACs' after the callsign used by the 612th's commander, Lt-Col 'Bud' Day, who happened to like Errol Garner's song *Misty*.

When the Misty FAC missions ended in the autumn of 1970, the aircrews involved had logged 21,000 hours of combat time. Long before then, the F-100F's pioneer work in this respect had been copied by other units. There was Wolf FAC, with F-4Ds from the 8th TFW at Ubon, Thailand; Stormy FAC, with F-4Ds from the 366th TFW at Da Nang; and Tiger FAC, using F-4Es of the 388th TFW, Korat, Thailand. The FAC crews were among the most courageous of the war, almost always having to operate in the teeth of intense anti-aircraft fire.

As mentioned earlier, many of the units flying combat with the F-100 in Vietnam were drawn from the Air National Guard. Five of these units – the 120th TFS, Colorado ANG, the 136th TFS, New York ANG, the 174th TFS, Iowa ANG, the 188th TFS, New Mexico ANG, and the 355th TFS (nominally an Air Force unit, but manned predominantly by ANG personnel) – were described by General George S. Brown, Chief of Staff of the United States Air Force from 1973, as the best F-100 units in Vietnam combat. There was no doubt that the Air Guard units, on average, flew more combat missions than the other squadrons at their bases, and generally achieved better results. Their aircraft were also better maintained – although, in common with other F-100 users in Vietnam, they had to contend with an ongoing spares problem.

The Air National Guard continued to operate F-100s until 1979, when the type at last began to be phased out of the USAF inventory. The last operational mission in a Super Sabre was flown on 10 November 1979 by Lt William D. Layne of the 113th TFS, 181st TFG, Terre Haute, Indiana. This sortie was made from Hulman Field in F-100D 56-2979, a twenty-three-year-old aircraft that had seen service in Vietnam. Soon afterwards, it was ferried by Brigadier-General Frank L. Hettlinger, commanding the 122nd TFW of the Indiana ANG, to the Military Aircraft Storage and Disposition Centre (MASDC) at Davis-Monthan AFB, Arizona. There, many of the F-100s were converted to pilotless target drones, to be shot down somewhat ingloriously by their own side.

Chapter 16
F-107A: Last of the Sabre Line

EARLY IN 1953, the USAF asked North American to initiate studies of an improved version of the F-100A, to be designated F-100B. The goal was to have the new variant in production by 1955. Initially, the design used the same wing planform as the F-100A, but with a five per cent thickness/chord ratio instead of the F-100A's seven per cent. The F-100B was to be powered by an uprated J57 engine developing 16,000 lb of thrust, which would give it an estimated top speed of 1.80M. A 1,160 gallon fuel load would be carried in wing tanks, no provision being made for external tanks, and dual landing-gear wheels would permit the aircraft to operate from unprepared strips.

North American also studied an all-weather interceptor version (variously known as the F-100I and F-100BI) which was to have a modified cockpit, radar AI equipment, rocket armament, heated wing leading edges and provision for external tanks.

While studies of this and the original air-superiority version were in progress, North American decided to investigate the F-100B's potential as a fighter-bomber, featuring six wing hardpoints and a number of structural changes. The Air Force was interested, and on 11 June 1954 North American received a letter contract authorizing the procurement of materials for thirty-three F-100B fighter-bombers. On 8 July came notification that production aircraft would be designated F-107A. By this time the powerplant intended for the new type had changed, the more powerful Pratt & Whitney J75 engine having become available.

The F-107A's primary weapon was to be the TX-28 nuclear store. To carry this weapon internally would have raised a number of structural design problems, so North American's engineers decided that it would have to be carried semi-recessed on the centreline of the fuselage belly. (This method of stowage was also adopted later on by Avions Marcel Dassault of France in the design of their nuclear bomber, the Mirage IV.) In the case of the F-107A, though, there was a snag which was only discovered when North American carried out wind-tunnel tests to check the release and separation of the weapon; the airflow from the nose radome and chin air intake combined to produce unacceptable inter-ference. NAA's solution was to move the intake to the top of the fuselage, immediately behind the cockpit, giving the design a unique appearance. The vertical tail surface was another design change, comprising a single-piece slab pivoting about an axis. A spoiler system of hinged doors on both the upper and lower wing surfaces controlled the airflow over the wings during high-speed manoeuvring.

The first F-107A (AF55-5118) flew on 10 September 1956 at Edwards AFB, with NAA chief test pilot Bob Baker at the controls. Baker climbed out at 0.92M then briefly went supersonic with military power in level flight before returning to land. During the approach with gear down, he found that full flap resulted in over-sensitive lateral control, so to reduce the rate of roll to a manageable level he retracted the flaps to about halfway and added ten knots to his airspeed. Unfortunately, the brake parachute malfunctioned on touchdown. Baker elected not to use hard braking to stop the aircraft, having three miles of concrete run-way with a further five miles of smooth dry lake bed beyond, but a rut caused the nose gear to collapse and the F-107A slid ignominiously to a stop. The damage was not substantial, and the aircraft was flying again three days later.

Three F-107As were built, the third having a variable air inlet duct, and the test programme was well under way when, in 1957, the USAF selected the Republic F-105 to meet its tactical fighter-bomber requirement. The first and third F-107As were turned over to NACA's High-Speed Flight Station at Edwards AFB for research work, and some of their design features – including the slab tail and the augmented longitudinal control system – were later incorporated in the North American A3J

Vigilante naval attack aircraft. Most of this work was done by the third F-107A, the first having been grounded after only four flights because of continual mechanical problems. The other aircraft was used to evaluate the sidestick controller that eventually went into the X-15 high-speed research aircraft; it made forty flights in 1958–9 before being damaged beyond economical repair during an aborted take-off.

The first F-107A is today in the Pima Air Museum, Tucson, Arizona, while the second aircraft (AF55-5119) may be seen in the Air Force Museum at Wright-Patterson AFB, Ohio.

Tailpiece:
The Sabre Lives On

FOUR DECADES after the F-86A fought for supremacy over North Korea, the Sabre story continues. The Canadair Sabre Mk 6 still flies in civilian colours with Flight Systems Inc, Mojave, towing target darts to provide gunnery practice for fighter pilots; others, lovingly maintained, survive as flying museum pieces, while others still, their numbers steadily dwindling, take to the air as QF-86 unmanned target drones, being mostly expended over the White Sands Missile Range. Many more exist around the world as static museum pieces and airfield gate guardians.

Six thousand two hundred and eight Sabres of all marks (554 F-86A, 336 E, 2,450 F, 473 H, 2,054 D and 341 K) were built by North American, Fiat and Mitsubishi. Canadair produced 1,815, and the Commonwealth Aircraft Corporation 113. Add to this 1,187 Furies of all marks, and you have an impressive total of 9,323.

It is for its role in the air war over Korea that the Sabre will be forever remembered in aviation history, but its value was immeasurably greater than that. It gave thousands of combat pilots around the world confidence in high-speed flight, nudging them through what the popular

Civil-registered Sabre Mk 6 N186F (ex-RCAF 23454) was used by Flight Test Research Inc, Long Beach, California, before going to Flight Systems Inc., Mojave.

Flight Systems Inc's Sabre Mk 6 N80FS (ex-*Luftwaffe* BB+284, KE+104), prepares for take-off from Tyndall AFB, California. The aircraft is carrying a dart-type towed target.

N80FS at Luke AFB Arizona on 25 October 1989, with F-15 Eagles in the background.

Sabre Mk 5 N86FS was RCAF 23367. It is seen here after landing at Tyndall AFB on 24 October 1990 after a gunnery sortie with F-15s. The dart target has been jettisoned.

Press termed the sound barrier; test pilots like Britain's Roland Beamont and America's Scott Crossfield – of X-15 fame – had their first taste of supersonic flight in an F-86.

Within NATO, the Sabre filled a dangerous gap in a Europe which, in the wake of the 1948–9 Berlin crisis, was being subjected to growing pressure from the Soviet Union. It was the right aircraft for the job; thanks to Korea, the Russians were well aware of its capabilities as a fighting machine; and, most important of all, it was available in sufficient numbers at the right time. Later, in two brief wars fought by Pakistan, it showed that it could still hold its own against equipment which, at least on paper, was far superior in terms of performance.

And, in common with other truly responsive fighter aircraft such as the Spitfire, Mustang and Hunter, it was beloved by everyone who flew it. It was an aircraft in which the pilot was very much in control of his destiny, lacking the benefits of the complex electronic systems that were the hallmark of later interceptors. The Sabre was one of the last true fighters.

The Confederate Air Force's F-86 Sabre, N3145T, pictured at a CAF air show at Midland/Odessa, Texas, 10 October 1992.

Strange bedfellows: Sabre Mk 6 and MiG-15, both belonging to Combat Jets Inc, show their paces together during the 'Wings over Houston' show at Ellington AFB, 2 October 1988.

F-86E Sabre 51-2897, in 51st FIW markings, belongs to Combat Jets Inc. It was photographed at Houston, Texas, on 3 October 1988. Note the nose art.

F-86D 53-1030, formerly of the Texas Air Guard, is now on display at the General Dynamics Air Park, Fort Worth, Texas.

Appendix: USAF F-86 Combat Wings – Deployments and Operations

1st Fighter Wing (FW). Later redesignated the 1st Tactical Fighter Wing (TFW), the 1st FW was the first to equip with the F-86A Sabre, beginning with the 9th Fighter Squadron (FS) in February 1949. By the end of May, the 27th and 71st Squadrons had also equipped. Based at March Air Force Base (AFB), California, the Wing moved to Norton AFB on 1 December 951 and was de-activated there on 6 February 1952. Its role was the air defence of southern California. Reactivated in 1956 and equipped with F-102 aircraft, it continued to use a number of F-86s for general purposes until 1960.

4th Fighter Wing (Later, 4th TFW). The 4th FW equipped with F-86A Sabres in 1949 at Wilmington (New Castle County Airport) and its three squadrons, the 334th, 335th and 336th, were assigned to the Eastern Air Defense Force. In December 1950 it deployed to Korea; a full account of its operations will be found in the main text. From 1953–57 the 4th TFW provided air defence and reconnaissance in Korea, Japan, Formosa and the Philippines, returning to the United States to re-equip with F-100s in December 1957.

8th Fighter-Bomber Wing (FBW) (Later, 8th TFW). The 8th FBW (35th, 36th and 80th Fighter Bomber Squadrons (FBS)) exchanged its F-80C Shooting Stars for F-86F Sabres from February 1953 and used these during the final phase of the Korean War. During 1953–54 the Wing was responsible for the air defence of southern Korea and for the maintenance of a quick reaction strike force, a role it continued to fulfil after re-equipping with F-100s in

1956–7. See main text for Korean operations.

18th Fighter-Bomber Wing (Later, 18th TFW). The 18th FBW – 12th and 67th FBS, with No 2 Sqn SAAF attached – began converting to the F-86F Sabre in January 1953 and used the aircraft on operations for the remainder of the Korean War (see main text). On 1 November 1954 the Wing moved to Okinawa, supporting tactical operations there and in Korea, Japan and Formosa. The 18th TFW began re-equipping with the F-100 in 1957. The 336th Fighter-Day Squadron was attached to the Wing from 7 August 1956 to 1 February 1957.

21st Fighter-Bomber Wing (Later, 21st TFW). The 21st FBW was activated at George AFB, California, on 1 January 1953 and equipped with F-86Fs. Assigned to the Ninth Air Force, its role was to maintain tactical proficiency and provide air defence augmentation in the United States. In December 1954 it moved to Chambley Air Base (AB), France, where it was assigned to the Twelfth Air Force. It performed special weapons tactical air operations as part of the NATO air defences in Europe. It continued to operate F-86Fs until 1958, when they were replaced by F-100s.

23rd Fighter Wing (Later, 23rd TFW). Based at Presque Isle AFB, Maine, the 23rd FW operated F-86E Sabres in 1951–2 and was responsible for the air defence of the north-eastern United States. The Sabre-equipped squadrons were the 132nd and 134th. The Wing also operated F-51s and F-80s during this period.

33rd Fighter Wing (Later, 33rd TFW). Equipped with F-86A Sabres, the 33rd FW assumed an air defence mission in 1949 and, based at Otis AFB, Mass., it provided air defence in the north-eastern United States until deactivated on 6 February 1952. The primary air defence mission was undertaken by the 58th, 59th and 60th Fighter Squadrons; the 133rd FS was also attached from July 1951 to February 1952. In 1956, the 33rd TFW re-equipped with F-89 Scorpions.

35th Fighter-Bomber Wing (Later, 35th TFW). Although the 35th FBW used the F-51 Mustang throughout the Korean War, its primary role was the air defence of Japan, the Sabres were assigned to it from time to time. The Wing was equipped completely with F-86F Sabres late in 1953, the aircraft being flown by the 39th, 40th and 339th FBS. The Wing was de-activated on 1 October 1957.

36th Fighter Wing (Later, 36th TFW). Tactically operational from August 1948, the 36th FW introduced the first Allied jet fighters to Europe in the post-war years, being equipped successively with F-80s, F-84s and – from 1953 to 1956 – with F-86F Sabres. Its Sabres, assigned to the Twelfth Air Force, were based at Bitburg, Germany. They were replaced by F-100s in 1956.

48th Fighter-Bomber Wing (Later, 48th TFW). Activated on 10 July 1952 and equipped initially with F-84 Thunderjets, the 48th FBW was assigned to the Twelfth Air Force and based at Chaumont AB, France. It received F-86F Sabres in 1953 and operated them until 1956, when they were replaced by F-100s. From June–November 1953 and July 1954–October 1956 the 48th FBW operated the USAFE *Skyblazers* aerobatic team.

49th Fighter-Bomber Wing (Later, 49th TFW). The 49th TFW operated F-84 Thunderjets throughout the Korean War, converting to F-86F Sabres in 1954. It assumed an air

defence mission in Japan with these aircraft until 1957, when it converted to F-100s. Squadrons attached during this period were the 4th, 7th, 8th, 39th, 334th, 336th and 339th Fighter-Interceptor Squadrons (FIS).

51st Fighter Wing (Later, 51st TFW). The 51st FW equipped with F-86E Sabres in 1951 and deployed to Korea for air superiority operations (see main text for full details). It remained in Korea after the end of hostilities to provide air defence until late July 1954, then assumed the air defence of the Ryukyu Islands, equipped with F-86Fs. From 29 August 1958 to 26 January 1959 one squadron deployed at Tainan, Formosa, during the Formosa Strait crisis. The F-86s flew numerous combat air patrols to provide cover for Nationalist Chinese Air Force flights resupplying besieged garrisons on Quemoy Island. The 51st TFW converted to F-102s in 1959, relinquishing the last of its Sabres in 1960.

56th Fighter Wing (Later, 56th TFW). The 56th FW (61st, 62nd and 63rd FIS) equipped with the F-86A Sabre early in 1950 and operated the type until 6 February 1952, when it was de-activated. Based at Selfridge AFB, Michigan, the Wing was responsible for the defence of a large portion of the north-eastern United States.

58th Fighter-Bomber Wing (Later, 58th Tactical Training Wing). Activated on 10 July 1952, the 58th FBW flew combat missions with F-84 Thunderjets until the end of hostilities in Korea, converting to F-86Fs at Taegu in 1954. It operated Sabres in the air defence of southern Korea until de-activation on 1 July 1958. Assigned fighter-bomber groups were the 49th, 58th and 474th; the 69th, 310th and 311th Fighter-Bomber Squadrons were also assigned in 1957–8.

67th Tactical Reconnaissance Wing (TRW). Activated in 1947, the 67th TRW operated a miscellany of reconnaissance types, including RF-86 Sabres during 1951–6. The

Wing operated intensively during the Korean War, afterwards remaining in Korea – and later in Japan – to provide reconnaissance facilities as required.

78th Fighter Wing (Air Defense). Having previously operated F-89 Scorpions in 1951–2, the 78th FW was reactivated on 18 October 1956 at Hamilton AFB, California, and was equipped with F-86Ds and F-89s for the air defence of the US Pacific coast area. F-102s were also added to the strength from 1957. The Sabres were withdrawn in 1958.

81st Fighter Wing (Later, 81st TFW). The 81st FW, activated on 1 May 1948, flew air defence operations in Hawaii with F-47s and F-80s until 1949, when it returned to the USA to re-equip with F-86A Sabres. In November 1949 it became part of the Western Air Defense Force's air defence structure, operating from Kirtland AFB, New Mexico and Moses Lake (later Larson) AFB, Washington, before moving to RAF Bentwaters, Suffolk, UK, in 1951. Until mid-1954 the 81st FW worked with RAF Fighter Command in the air defence role, after which it converted to F-84Fs and changed from fighter-interceptor to fighter-bomber operations, armed with both conventional and tactical nuclear weapons.

83rd Fighter-Day Wing. Activated on 8 July 1956, the 83rd FDW was assigned to the Ninth Air Force, equipped with F-86H Sabres, and based at Seymour Johnson AFB, North Carolina. It converted to F-100Cs late in 1957.

86th Fighter Wing (Later, 86th TFW). The 86th FW was activated at Neubiberg AB, West Germany, on 1 July 1948 and was equipped initially with F-47 Thunderbolts. In August 1952, having re-equipped with F-84 Thunderjets two years earlier, it moved to Landstuhl (later Ramstein) AB, where it received F-86D Sabres in 1953. The Wing's primary role was air defence as part of the US Twelfth Air Force. The Sabre

remained in first-line use until 1960, when the 86th equipped with more modern types (F-100, F-102, F-104) and was given Air Division Status. Squadrons attached to the 86th FW during 1953–60 were the 440th, 496th, 512th, 513th, 514th, 525th, 526th and 527th FIS.

312th Fighter-Bomber Wing (Later, 312th TFW). The 312th FBW was activated at Clovis (later Cannon) AFB, New Mexico, on 1 October 1954 and equipped with F-86H Sabres. Assigned to the Ninth Air Force, its task was to maintain proficiency in fighter-bomber operations with conventional weapons. From April 1956 to October 1957, by which time it had also received some F-100s, it rotated tactical squadrons to France, six months at a time, and trained to maintain combat proficiency with nuclear weapons. The Wing was de-activated on 18 February 1959.

323rd Fighter-Bomber Wing. Based at Bunker Hill AFB, Indiana, the 323rd FBW was essentially a tactical operational training unit, and was equipped with Sabres (F-86F/H) in 1955–7. It was de-activated on 1 September 1957.

325th Fighter Wing (Air Defense). Originally established in May 1948 as the 325th Fighter Wing, All Weather, the 325th was redesignated on 14 September 1956 and equipped with F-86D Sabres at McChord AFB, Washington. Squadrons attached or assigned to the Wing were the 317th, 318th and 498th. The Sabres were replaced by F-102s from 1957. The Wing's operational task was the air defence of the US west coast.

366th Fighter-Bomber Wing (Later, 366th TFW). Activated at Alexandria (later England) AFB, Louisiana, on 1 January 1953, the 366th FBW was equipped with F-86F/H Sabres until 1955, when the F-84F Thunderstreak became its primary equipment. The Wing rotated tactical squadrons to France and Italy.

388th Fighter-Bomber Wing (Later, 388th TFW). Originally established as the 388th Fighter-Day Wing in March 1953, this unit was redesignated the 388th FBW on 5 November that year. It operated F-86F Sabres from 1954 to 1957, training in the fighter-bomber role at Clovis (later Cannon) AFB, New Mexico, before moving to Etain-Rouvres AB, France, on 12 December 1954. The 388th FBW took part in NATO operations and exercises before being replaced by the 49th FBW in December 1957, after which it was de-activated. Personnel returned to the United States for training on F-100 and F-105 aircraft.

406th Fighter-Interceptor Wing (FIW). Equipped with F-86D Sabres, the 406th FIW (87th, 512th, 513th and 514th FIS) became established in the all-weather air defence role at RAF Manston, Kent, in November 1953, coming under the operational control of RAF Fighter Command. In addition to providing all-weather air defence for the United Kingdom, the 406th deployed squadrons to Soesterberg AB, in the Netherlands, in 1954–55. The Wing was de-activated on 15 May 1958.

Index